# Power & Ethics

## A Brief History Of Western Moral and Political Philosophy

Waleed Mahmud

In memory of my beloved brother,
*Mashal,*

And

For my *Parents and Partner*,
who always nurtured the writer within me

# Table of Contents

**Preface** ........................................................................................................................5
**Chapter 1: Moral and Political Philosophy** ...............................................................6
**Chapter 2: The Historical Imperative** .....................................................................11
**Chapter 3: The Greek Era (~600 BCE to ~500 CE)** .................................................14
    i. Socrates (470 BCE - 399 BCE) ..........................................................................15
    ii. Plato (427 BCE - 347 BCE) ...............................................................................18
    iii. Aristotle (384 BCE - 322 BCE) .........................................................................21
    IV. The Sophists (~500 BCE to ~400 BCE) ..........................................................24
    V. Diogenes and the Cynics (~400 BCE to ~320 BCE) ........................................27
    VI. Zeno and the Stoics (336 BCE - 265 BCE) .....................................................30
    VII. Epicurus and the Epicureans (341 BCE - 270 BCE) ......................................33
    VIII. Pyrrho and the Skeptics (360 BCE to 270 BCE) ...........................................36
**Chapter 4: The Late Antiquity to the Medieval Period** ..........................................39
    i. The Late Antiquity (~300 CE to ~800 CE) ..........................................................40
    ii. The Islamic Golden Age (~800 CE to ~1300 CE) ..............................................43
    iii. The Jewish Philosophical Tradition (~1100 CE to ~1200 CE) ..........................46
    IV. The Medieval Scholastics (~1100 CE to ~1600 CE) ........................................49
**Chapter 5: Renaissance (~1300 CE to ~1600 CE)** ..................................................53
    i. Giovanni Pico della Mirandola (1463–1494) ......................................................54
    ii. Desiderius Erasmus (1466–1536) .....................................................................56
    iii. Niccolò Machiavelli (1469–1527) ......................................................................58
    IV. Michel de Montaigne (1533–1592) ...................................................................60
    V. Thomas Hobbes (1588 CE - 1679 CE) .............................................................62
**Chapter 6: Enlightenment (~1600 CE to ~1800 CE)** ...............................................64
    Enlightenment's Influence on Society and Governance .......................................65
    i. John Locke (1632–1704) ....................................................................................67
    ii. Voltaire (1694–1778) .........................................................................................69
    iii. Jean-Jacques Rousseau (1712–1778) .............................................................70
    IV. David Hume (1711–1776) ................................................................................72
    V. Adam Smith (1723–1790) .................................................................................74
    VI. Immanuel Kant (1724–1804) ............................................................................75
    VII. Jeremy Bentham (1748–1832) ........................................................................77
    VIII. Edmund Burke (1729–1797) ..........................................................................79
    Modern Critiques on the Enlightenment ...............................................................80
**Chapter 7: Age of Revolutions (19th to 20th Century)** ..........................................86
    i. John Stuart Mill (1806 - 1873) ............................................................................88
    ii. Karl Marx (1818 - 1883) ....................................................................................89
    iii. Søren Kierkegaard (1813 - 1855) .....................................................................91

    IV. Friedrich Nietzsche (1844 - 1900) ........................................................................ 92
    V. The Abolition of Slavery ........................................................................................ 93
    VI. The Suffrage Movement ....................................................................................... 95
    VII. The Early Labor Movement ................................................................................. 97

**Chapter 8: Modern and Postmodern Era (>1900 CE) ................................................. 99**
    i. Existentialism and Humanism in the Contemporary Era ....................................... 101
    ii. Postmodernism and Critiques of Meta-Narratives ............................................... 105
    iii. Feminism and Gender Theory ............................................................................ 108
    IV. Environmental Philosophy and Ethics ............................................................... 111
    V. Philosophical Responses to Technological Change .......................................... 115
    VI. Globalization and Multiculturalism ..................................................................... 119

**Chapter 9: Contemporary Challenges & Innovations ............................................ 123**

**Epilogue ........................................................................................................................ 126**

**Glossary ....................................................................................................................... 127**

**List of References and Further Readings .............................................................. 129**

# Preface

As I initiate the journey of penning "*Power & Ethics: A Brief History Of Western Moral and Political Philosophy,*" my thoughts gravitate towards the profound explorations that began with my earlier work, "Probing Freewill." The rich conversations of free will and determinism, which first unraveled in that volume, form an integral part of this expansive series on moral and political philosophy. This book, while serving as the foundational volume, ushers in a broader discourse intended to bridge ancient philosophical wisdom with the pressing challenges of the contemporary world.

Crafted with both the academic and the curious mind at heart, this book is structured to guide the reader through the vast epochs of philosophical thought. We begin in the chasms of ancient Greece and travel through the medieval period, the Renaissance, and the Enlightenment, culminating in modern and postmodern philosophies. Each chapter is dedicated to one era, distilling its essence and examining its contributions to the moral and political dialogues that shape our current ethos.

The significance of this book lies not only in its historical analysis but in its role as a precursor to future volumes that will delve into the philosophical challenges and responses of our time, including issues of globalization, ethical dilemmas posed by climate change, AI, privacy, social justice, and the overarching influence of technological advancements on morality and politics. It aims to serve as the bedrock for subsequent discussions, providing readers with the foundational knowledge necessary to appreciate the depth of future explorations.

This series is designed to be more than a recount of philosophical milestones. It is an invitation to engage actively with the questions and ideas that continue to shape our collective human experience. As we traverse from the theories of free will and determinism to the expansive debates on social justice and political philosophy, this book endeavors to illuminate the paths we choose today and the ways they are informed by the philosophical insights of the past.

In crafting this discourse, I have strived to maintain clarity and accessibility, ensuring that the philosophical explorations within these pages resonate not only with scholars but with anyone intrigued by the ethical dimensions of contemporary life. The language chosen is deliberate, designed to engage, provoke thought, and inspire action. This book is not merely to be read but is an invitation to reflect, challenge the status quo, and perhaps even redefine our understanding of the good life. As we step into the complexities of our times, let this book serve as a beacon of wisdom and courage, a guide towards a more just, equitable, and enlightened society. Let us embark on this intellectual odyssey together, arming ourselves with the insights of the past to navigate the uncertainties of the future.

> ***"The journey of philosophical discovery is not just about understanding the world but about transforming it."***

Let this series inspire you to think critically, act justly, and live meaningfully, as we continue to shape the world with the clarity and freedom that comes from profound philosophical insight and a heartfelt commitment to the betterment of humanity.

# Chapter 1: Moral and Political Philosophy

**Moral philosophy**, or ethics, deals with the questions of right and wrong, good and bad, just and unjust. It concerns itself with the justification of actions, the virtues of character, and the foundational principles of moral conduct. Since the inception of society, this has been a central pursuit of human thought, influencing how we navigate our daily lives. Ancient Greek philosophers like Plato and Aristotle viewed morality through the lens of virtue, Medieval and Renaissance thinkers, influenced by religious doctrines, intertwined morality with spiritual salvation, and the Enlightenment Era emphasized moral principles that could be discerned through rational thought.

In the 19th and 20th centuries, the emergence of utilitarianism and existentialist ethics reflected an increasingly complex world, where the consequences of actions and individual freedom became central concerns. Existentialists, such as Jean-Paul Sartre, emphasized the individual's responsibility in creating meaning and values in an indifferent universe, as articulated in works like "Being and Nothingness." Today, the discourse on morality is enriched by discussions on bioethics, environmental ethics, and the ethics of technology, reflecting new challenges posed by advancements in science and technology. Questions about genetic engineering, artificial intelligence, and environmental sustainability illustrate how our moral considerations continue to evolve in response to changing realities.

**Political philosophy**, the contemplative twin of moral philosophy, peaks into the principles underlying the organization and governance of societies. It not only asks what makes a government legitimate but also probes the rights and obligations of individuals within societies, the just distribution of resources, and the nature of justice, authority, and the state itself. Its significance lies in its capacity to frame the blueprints for societal structures, not only influencing the abstract realm of ideas but the concrete realities of communal life.

At its core, political philosophy endeavors to define the ideal state and the best form of government, guiding societies in their quest for good governance and social harmony, by providing ideological underpinnings for political systems and institutions. From Plato's "Republic," envisioning a society ruled by philosopher-kings, to John Locke's treatises advocating for natural rights and government by consent, the visions of political philosophy have long shaped the foundations upon which modern democracies are built. For instance, the concept of the social contract, championed by Rousseau, Hobbes, and Locke, introduced the idea that the legitimacy of state authority derives from the consent of the governed, laying the groundwork for modern democratic governance. Similarly, Karl Marx's critique of capitalism and his vision of a classless society have influenced political movements and economic policies around the globe.

In today's globalized world, political philosophy plays an integral role in addressing the challenges of democracy and governance. As nations navigate issues like economic inequality, migration, climate change, and the rise of populism, political philosophy offers insights into balancing the demands of justice, freedom, and security. The question of how to achieve a fair and equitable distribution of resources, for example, draws on theories of justice from Rawls to Nozick, highlighting the ongoing debate between egalitarian and libertarian philosophies.

Globalization, with its transnational flows of people, goods, and ideas, poses unique challenges to the traditional notions of sovereignty and national governance. Political philosophy aids in rethinking governance in an interconnected world, contemplating supranational entities like the European Union or the United Nations, or the complexities of international law and human rights. Political philosophy remains crucial for organizing society and guiding its evolution, equipping citizens and leaders alike with the critical tools needed to evaluate the ethical foundations of political actions and policies, encouraging a more informed and reflective participation in the public sphere.

Moral philosophy, with its focus on what constitutes right action and virtuous living, inevitably spills over into the realm of political philosophy, which contemplates the organization and governance of societies, reflecting a relationship that has evolved over centuries of philosophical inquiry. While each domain addresses distinct aspects of human thought and society, they are united by their foundational pursuit of understanding the good life and the just society. This overlap is most evident in discussions about justice and rights, where moral judgments about what is fair or equitable inform political theories about law, governance, and social structures.

***Can moral philosophy exist independently of political considerations?*** To some extent, yes. One can contemplate personal ethics and moral virtues without directly engaging with political structures or theories. For example, one might consider the ethics of honesty or compassion in personal relationships without invoking political concepts. Conversely, political philosophy can also be seen as possessing its distinct realm, focusing on issues of power, governance, and the structure of societies, which do not always directly engage with questions of personal morality. Political philosophers might debate the merits of different forms of government or the nature of political obligations without directly addressing the moral virtues of individuals within those societies. However, the separation is not absolute. Political decisions and structures deeply impact the moral choices available to individuals, and moral convictions often drive political action and theories about governance. Thus, while they can be considered independently to some extent, moral and political philosophy are deeply interconnected, each informing and shaping the other.

The intersection of moral and political philosophy is most pronounced in their joint exploration of justice, equity, and freedom, concepts that demand both ethical reasoning and political organization for their realization. Justice, as a moral virtue, requires not only personal adherence to fairness but also political systems that ensure equitable treatment under the law. Political philosophies that define justice in terms of rights, duties, or the distribution of resources draw heavily on moral principles to justify their positions. Similarly, equity and freedom are concepts that bridge the individual and the collective, demanding moral consideration of what individuals owe to each other and political action to structure societies in ways that enable equitable access to freedoms. Theories of distributive justice, for example, navigate this intersection by considering what constitutes a fair distribution of resources (a moral question) and how political institutions can be organized to achieve this distribution (a political question).

Today, the relevance of moral and political philosophy stems from their capacity to provide deep insights into the human condition, ethics, and the principles of just governance. As society grapples with the implications of digital technology, artificial intelligence, and environmental degradation, these philosophical domains offer essential tools for critical reflection and informed decision-making. The rapid pace of technological innovation, particularly in the fields of artificial intelligence (AI) and digital communication, presents novel ethical challenges that cannot be adequately addressed by traditional moral and political frameworks alone. Issues such as data privacy, surveillance, and the ethical use of AI in decision-making processes raise questions about autonomy, consent, and the moral status of artificial entities. Moral philosophy urges us to consider the values that should guide our interactions with these technologies, while political philosophy explores how governance structures can regulate their use to protect individual rights and promote the common good.

Similarly, the escalating ecological crises exemplified by climate change, biodiversity loss, and resource depletion demand a reevaluation of our moral responsibilities to the planet and future generations. Moral philosophy challenges us to extend our ethical considerations to non-human entities and ecosystems, reconceptualizing notions of stewardship and intergenerational justice. Political philosophy, on the other hand, provides a framework for reimagining governance models that can address these global challenges, fostering cooperation across nations and creating policies that balance economic development with environmental sustainability.

The deployment of AI systems in various sectors, from healthcare to criminal justice, presents ethical dilemmas regarding fairness, accountability, and the potential displacement of human labor. Moral philosophy prompts us to consider the ethical implications of delegating critical decisions to machines, emphasizing the importance of transparency, justice, and human oversight. Political philosophy, meanwhile, explores the regulatory frameworks needed to ensure that AI technologies serve the public interest, advocating for policies that mitigate risks and distribute benefits equitably. The digital age has radically transformed our notions of privacy and consent, as personal data becomes an increasingly valuable commodity. Moral philosophy encourages a critical examination of the rights to privacy and autonomy in the face of pervasive data collection and surveillance technologies. Political philosophy examines the role of the state and international bodies in protecting these rights, calling for robust legal protections that safeguard individuals' privacy while enabling the beneficial uses of digital technologies.

The timeless insights of great philosophers, from Socrates to Confucius, provide a blanket of wisdom that, though conceived in vastly different contexts, remains profoundly relevant to the challenges we face today. The application of ancient ethics to contemporary challenges is not about prescribing direct solutions but rather about adopting a philosophical lens through which to view and assess modern dilemmas. For instance, Aristotle's concept of the "Golden Mean," the virtuous path between two extremes, can be applied to debates surrounding digital consumption, advocating for a balanced approach that neither eschews technology altogether nor succumbs uncritically to its allure. Similarly, the Stoic emphasis on inner tranquility and control over one's responses to external events offers valuable insights into handling the stress and uncertainty of modern life. In an age characterized by rapid change and information overload, Stoicism teaches the importance of focusing on what is within our control, encouraging a resilience that is deeply needed in contemporary society.

For instance, drawing on the Stoic view of humans as custodians of the earth, modern environmental ethics can be informed by a sense of duty to protect and preserve the natural world for future generations, reinforcing the importance of sustainable living and environmental responsibility in the face of climate change and biodiversity loss. Similarly, Plato's allegory of the cave, where prisoners mistook shadows for reality, mirrors today's challenges in distinguishing between authentic experiences and digital facades. This can spark critical reflections on the impact of social media on our perception of reality and the value of seeking truth beyond the digital shadows that often captivate our attention. Concurrently, the Socratic method of dialogue and questioning remains a powerful tool for education and personal growth, encouraging critical thinking and ethical inquiry in an era often dominated by dogmatism and polarized debates.

Through the rigors of philosophical inquiry, we not only gain knowledge, but a transformative understanding that empowers us to confront and address societal challenges at their very core. It encourages a questioning attitude towards accepted norms and inspires us to envision alternative futures grounded in ethical principles. Philosophical debates on justice and equity have propelled movements for social change, influencing policies on civil rights, gender equality, and social welfare. For example, the civil rights movement in the United States, grounded in the ethical principles of equality and human dignity, showcases how philosophical ideals can mobilize mass action towards societal change. Martin Luther King Jr., influenced by the nonviolent philosophy of Gandhi and the ethical teachings of Jesus, led a movement that fundamentally transformed American society by challenging and dismantling institutionalized racial segregation and discrimination.

At the individual level, philosophical inquiry fosters a sense of moral responsibility that extends beyond personal interests to the broader implications of our societal footprints. The study of ethics, with its emphasis on virtues, duties, and consequences, equips us with the ability to discern right from wrong in complex situations. For instance, consider Kant's categorical imperative that one should act only in accordance with those maxims through which you can, at the same time, will that it become a universal law. This principle challenges individuals to consider the universality of their actions, promoting a form of ethical reasoning that discourages selfishness and garners a sense of duty towards others. Consider the philosophical discussions around punishment, rehabilitation, and the nature of justice have inspired reforms in criminal justice systems. The adoption of restorative justice practices, which focus on the rehabilitation of offenders through reconciliation with victims and the community at large, reflects a philosophical shift towards a more humane and effective approach to criminal justice, emphasizing healing over punitive measures.

A deeper understanding of moral and political philosophy not only enlightens us but can also galvanize us to pursue societal transformation. The teachings of philosophers like John Rawls, who envisioned a society where social and economic inequalities are arranged to benefit the least advantaged, offer a powerful vision for restructuring our social institutions towards greater justice. Rawls' theory of justice as fairness illustrates how philosophical concepts can inspire legislative and social reforms aimed at reducing inequality and improving social mobility. For example, the environmental movement, driven by ethical concerns about humanity's relationship with the natural world, draws heavily on philosophical concepts of stewardship, intergenerational justice, and the intrinsic value of nature. Philosophers like Peter Singer and Aldo Leopold have been instrumental in articulating the moral imperatives for environmental conservation, inspiring global efforts to combat climate change and protect biodiversity.

As we stand on the precipice of starting this discourse, it becomes evident that this is not just an academic exercise but a crucial undertaking for anyone navigating through life. The exploration of these philosophical domains is imperative, not just for the scholar but for every one of us. The reason for this necessity is eloquently captured in the words of Nathaniel Branden, who recounts an encounter in his lecture on The Basic Principles of Objectivism:

*"I once… engaged in an argument about free enterprise versus collectivism. The man… declared that he had no interest in philosophy, that all theories were nonsense, and that abstract ideas had nothing to do with actual life… that everything I was saying might have been true in the 19th century but after all we are living in the 20th century and what was true yesterday is not true today… There is no such thing as a fixed permanent reality… only constant (is) change. He did not know that he was offering a metaphysical view of reality, first promulgated in western civilization 2500 Years ago by a philosopher named Heraclitus, who taught it to Hegel, who taught it to John Dewey, who taught it to his students, who taught it to the writers of the newspaper editorials, who taught it to the comic strips, who taught it to this gentleman."*

This anecdote serves as a powerful reminder that, whether we acknowledge it or not, our thoughts, beliefs, and arguments are deeply imbued with philosophical underpinnings. One might profess indifference to philosophy, yet in the very act of dismissal, engage in a philosophical stance. The principles and ideas of moral and political philosophy permeate our lives, shaping our understanding of justice, freedom, rights, and the good life, even if we do not consciously recognize their influence.

The importance of consciously engaging with moral and political philosophy, rather than unconsciously absorbing fragmented and perhaps distorted versions of these philosophies, cannot be overstated. By actively exploring these fields, we equip ourselves with the tools to critically examine the foundations of our beliefs and the structures of our societies. We empower ourselves to make informed decisions, to engage in meaningful debates, and to contribute to the shaping of a world that reflects our most deeply held values. Learning about moral and political philosophy is, therefore, not an optional endeavor reserved for the philosopher or the academic. It is a fundamental pursuit for anyone who seeks to live a thoughtful and examined life in our ever-changing world. By consciously engaging with these ideas, we not only enrich our understanding but also ensure that we are active participants in the ongoing dialogue that shapes our collective future. Let us, therefore, approach this journey with open minds and a keen awareness of the relevance and urgency of these philosophical explorations.

# Chapter 2: The Historical Imperative

The odyssey from ancient philosophy to the contemporary era marks not just the evolution of human thought but the very foundation upon which our modern moral and political topography is constructed. This journey through epochs of brilliance, conflict, and enlightenment, embodies the essence of human inquiry into the nature of good governance, justice, and the virtuous life. The significance of ancient philosophy in shaping modern thought cannot be overstated; it is here, amidst the dialogues of Socrates, the treatises of Aristotle, and the reflections of Machiavelli, that the bedrock of contemporary ethics and politics was laid.

The historical continuum of philosophical inquiry is a testament to humanity's unyielding pursuit of wisdom and understanding. Each era, from the ancient Greeks to the Renaissance humanists, contributed unique insights that cumulatively enriched our moral and political understanding. This enduring quest reflects an intrinsic aspect of the human condition: the drive to seek answers to fundamental questions about our nature, our society, and the principles that should guide our collective life.

The ancients grappled with questions of justice, virtue, and the ideal state, laying down ethical frameworks that continue to influence contemporary discourse. The medieval period, with its synthesis of classical philosophy and religious doctrine, forged new pathways in moral thought, addressing the nature of human free will and divine providence. The Renaissance, a rebirth of classical ideals amidst emerging arts and sciences, brought a renewed focus on human potential, dignity, and the nuances of political power. This historical journey is not merely a chronological account of philosophical development but a narrative that accentuates the profound impact of these ideas on the modern world. The principles articulated by Plato and Aristotle, for example, serve as cornerstones for current debates on justice, ethics, and the role of the state. The Stoic emphasis on virtue, resilience, and the common good resonates with contemporary pursuits of personal development and social responsibility. Similarly, the political realism of Machiavelli, challenging the idealism of earlier political theories, introduces a pragmatic approach to governance and power that echoes in the corridors of modern statesmanship. The humanistic ideals of the Renaissance, celebrating human reason and creativity, inspire ongoing efforts to balance tradition with innovation, authority with individual freedom.

The Enlightenment, emerging from the shadows of medieval scholasticism, ignited a transformative wave across Europe, championing the power of human reason as the primary source of knowledge and truth. Philosophers like John Locke, Immanuel Kant, and Jean-Jacques Rousseau critically examined the nature of human understanding, the rights of individuals, and the principles underpinning just and equitable societies. Locke's treatises on government posits that legitimate political authority is derived from the consent of the governed, a radical departure from the divine right of kings, laying foundational ideas for modern democracy. Kant's critical philosophy, encapsulating his famous dictum "Sapere aude!" ("Dare to know!"), encourages individuals to escape their self-imposed immaturity through the application of reason. Rousseau's discourse on inequality and social contracts explores the complexities of freedom and justice, offering profound insights into the tensions between individual liberties and communal obligations.

However, the Enlightenment's emphasis on reason and progress also sowed the seeds of discontents that unfolded in the modern era. The Industrial Revolution, while a testament to human ingenuity and the capacity to reshape the world, brought about social upheavals, highlighting the limitations of Enlightenment ideals in addressing the complexities of industrial and post-industrial societies. These discontents paved the way for modern philosophical reflections, where figures like Friedrich Nietzsche, Karl Marx, and Sigmund Freud offered critiques of Enlightenment rationalism, questioning the foundations of morality, the dynamics of economic structures, and the nature of the human psyche. Nietzsche's proclamation of the "death of God" challenged the Enlightenment's faith in reason and progress, suggesting that the loss of religious absolutes left humanity adrift in a sea of nihilism. Marx's analysis of capitalism and class struggle underscores the economic underpinnings of social relations and political power, critiquing the Enlightenment's neglect of material conditions. Freud's psychoanalytic theory unveiled the unconscious forces shaping human behavior, complicating the Enlightenment view of the rational, autonomous subject.

The journey through philosophical thought does not end with the modern era but extends into postmodern reflections, where the certainties of the Enlightenment and the grand narratives of modernity are further deconstructed. Postmodern thinkers like Michel Foucault, Jacques Derrida, and Jean-François Lyotard challenge the notions of universal truth, stable identity, and linear progress, advocating for a recognition of the plurality of perspectives, the constructed nature of knowledge, and the play of power in the creation of social realities. Foucault's analysis of discourse and power reveals how knowledge is intertwined with power relations, shaping social institutions and individual identities. Derrida's deconstruction critiques the logocentrism of Western thought, revealing the inherent instabilities and contradictions in texts. Lyotard's skepticism towards grand narratives highlights the fragmentation and diversity of post-industrial societies, questioning the viability of universal theories of progress or liberation.

These instances illustrate the evolving landscape of philosophical inquiry and its profound implications for contemporary moral and political thought. The ethical dilemmas posed by advancements in technology, the governance challenges of a globalized world, and the quest for social justice and equity, all find their precursors in the dialogues of ancient Athens, the courts of medieval Christendom, and the city-states of Renaissance Italy. Further, the Enlightenment's championing of reason, the modern critique of rationalism and social structures, and the postmodern challenge to universality and coherence, collectively enrich our understanding of the human condition. They remind us that the quest for knowledge, justice, and the good life is a dynamic and ongoing journey, reflecting the complexities, contradictions, and possibilities of the human experience.

Simultaneous to this discussion is the imperative to know that philosophy has not developed in isolation; rather, it has continuously interacted with, influenced, and been influenced by other fields of study. This interdisciplinarity is essential for a fuller understanding of the role of philosophy in shaping and reflecting broader cultural and intellectual currents. Here, we explore three primary areas of interaction with regards to philosophical history: science, technology, and the arts.

The relationship between philosophy and science is foundational, with the former often providing the conceptual groundwork for the development of scientific ideas. Philosophical inquiry into the nature of knowledge and reality has paved the way for scientific methodology. For instance, the philosophical work of René Descartes and his method of systematic doubt laid the groundwork for the scientific method, emphasizing the importance of questioning assumptions and relying on empirical evidence. Moreover, the discussions on causality by David Hume influenced the development of statistical and probabilistic thinking in scientific research. In modern times, philosophical debates about the interpretations of quantum mechanics, such as the Copenhagen interpretation versus multiverse theories, show the ongoing influence of philosophical thought in cutting-edge scientific fields. These debates revolve around the philosophical implications of scientific theories, such as determinism, reality, and the nature of knowledge.

In terms of technology, philosophical questions surrounding human-technology interaction have become increasingly significant. Philosophers like Martin Heidegger and more recently, Luciano Floridi, have explored the ethical, ontological, and epistemological dimensions of technology. Heidegger's concept of "enframing" describes the way technology can limit the ways in which we see the world, warning against viewing everything merely as a resource for exploitation. Furthermore, as artificial intelligence and robotics advance, philosophical discussions concerning consciousness, freewill, and the ethics of AI are critical. These discussions influence the development of technology, guiding it towards ethical implementations and considerations of human values.

Lastly, the arts have long been a medium for exploring and expressing philosophical ideas. Philosophical aesthetics, for instance, examines the nature and experience of beauty and artistic expression. The works of philosophers like Immanuel Kant and Arthur Schopenhauer have profoundly influenced theories of perception, emotion, and the sublime in art. Moreover, contemporary philosophical discussions about the interpretation of art and the role of the artist in society reflect ongoing debates in the philosophy of art. For example, the Dada and Surrealist movements were deeply influenced by Nietzsche's ideas on nihilism and the absurd, using art to challenge traditional values and explore new ways of seeing the world.

As we conclude this chapter on the historical imperative of philosophy, it is crucial to recognize that the journey through philosophical thought is not merely a linear progression but a discourse around diverse human experience and intellect. From the ancient Athenians to Renaissance Europe and Enlightenment thinkers, philosophy has continuously engaged with and shaped the fundamental notions of existence, ethics, and governance. This ongoing dialogue between past and present, between philosophical ideas and societal realities, demonstrates philosophy's enduring relevance. It is a testament to the power of philosophical inquiry to illuminate the complexities of human life and to guide us in our quest for justice, understanding, and the good life. Moving forward, let us carry with us the lessons of history, mindful of the profound impact philosophical thought has had, and continues to have, on human civilization.

# Chapter 3: The Greek Era (~600 BCE to ~500 CE)

The Greek Philosophical Era spanned across a millenia, marking a defining epoch in human history and transitioning from a world illuminated by myth to one explored through reason. This era stands as a beacon of human inquiry, heralding the dawn of Western thought and profoundly shaping the philosophical frameworks that underpin our contemporary understanding. Prior to this transformative period, societies were enmeshed in mythological ideals that provided cosmological explanations, moral guidance, and social frameworks, all originating from tales of divine interventions, heroic endeavors, and cosmic order.

The genesis of Greek philosophical thought represented a seismic shift from reliance on mythological narratives to a rigorous pursuit of knowledge grounded in reasoned discourse and empirical evidence. This evolution from myth to logic wasn't merely a change in intellectual curiosity but a fundamental transformation in the way humans perceived their place in the cosmos and sought to understand the principles governing reality, morality, and human conduct.

The pioneering figures of this era, like Thales, who sought natural explanations for the phenomena of the world, and Pythagoras, whose work at the intersection of mysticism and mathematics laid the groundwork for future scientific inquiry, marked the early stirrings of this intellectual revolution. Yet, it was the triumvirate of Socrates, Plato, and Aristotle that brought this movement to its zenith, each contributing in rich and distinct ways to Western philosophy.

Socrates, with his relentless pursuit of truth through the dialectical method, encouraged a critical examination of virtues, ethics, and knowledge itself, challenging the Athenian citizenry to reflect deeply on their beliefs and moral convictions. Plato, extending beyond his mentor's inquiry, constructed a vast philosophical edifice through his dialogues, delving into the realms of justice, the ideal state, the nature of reality, and the immortal essence of the soul. Aristotle, a polymath and Plato's most illustrious student, expanded the horizons of philosophical inquiry even further, laying down comprehensive treatises on ethics, politics, metaphysics, biology, and more, setting the stage for centuries of intellectual exploration.

The reverberations of the Greek Philosophical Era extend far beyond the historical confines of antiquity, infusing the very core of modern philosophical inquiry. Contemporary ethical debates, political dilemmas, and existential questions trace their lineage back to the ancient agora of Athens, reflecting the enduring legacy of Greek philosophy. As the medieval and Renaissance periods built upon and refined these ancient insights, the foundational principles of Greek thought became woven into the very fabric of Western civilization, underscoring the timeless quest for wisdom, truth, and an understanding of the human condition.

This era, then, is not just a chapter in the annals of history but a living dialogue that continues to resonate through the ages, challenging us to ponder the ethical, political, and metaphysical questions that define our collective journey in search of meaning and understanding.

# i. Socrates (470 BCE - 399 BCE)

Socrates, a foundational figure in Western philosophy, marked a decisive shift from the cosmological and naturalistic inquiries of his predecessors to a profound engagement with the human condition. His method and philosophical inquiries laid the groundwork for what would become the central themes of Western thought: ethics, politics, and the pursuit of knowledge. Unlike earlier philosophers such as Thales, Pythagoras, Anaximenes, and Anaximander, who concentrated on understanding the physical world, Socrates focused on exploring internal virtues and societal values, setting the stage for an enduring philosophical discourse.

At the core of Socratic philosophy is the dialectical method, also known as **the Socratic Method**. This approach is characterized by its use of rigorous questioning to deconstruct and understand complex concepts such as justice, virtue, and the essence of the good life. Socrates pioneered this method as a form of pedagogical dialogue, wherein he engaged his interlocutors in probing philosophical discussions that encouraged them to question their presuppositions and arrive at deeper truths through their own reasoning.

This method was revolutionary not only in its approach to knowledge acquisition but also in its implications for democratic discourse. Socrates regularly engaged with the citizens of Athens in public places, inviting them to re-evaluate the norms of their society and reflect critically on their beliefs. His approach was not about teaching knowledge straightforwardly but developing a critical and reflective mindset that empowered individuals to discern ethical truths and cultivate moral virtues autonomously.

Central to his teaching was the notion that virtue is inherently connected to knowledge. Socrates famously asserted that **to know the good is to do the good**; that is, if one truly understands what is right, one's actions will naturally align with that understanding. This conflation of knowledge and ethical behavior invites a deeper examination of the nature of morality and the capacity for moral judgment. It presupposes that moral errors are a result of ignorance rather than malice, a view that suggests a radical rethinking of responsibility and ethical conduct.

This perspective resonates with modern philosophical explorations into the nature of freedom of choice, such as those discussed in my previous book, that question the underpinnings of free will and moral responsibility. If all wrongful actions are the result of ignorance, the role of education, and by extension, philosophy, becomes central to the cultivation of a just and moral society.

Socrates' scrutiny of Athenian democracy brought to light several paradoxes within the democratic system. His criticisms were not aimed at the concept of democracy itself but at the unexamined assumptions upon which Athenian democracy operated. He was skeptical of the notion that all opinions are equal and argued that true political leadership should be based on wisdom and insight rather than popularity or majority rule. This skepticism is evident in his dialogues, where he often challenged the qualifications of those deemed wise by the populace, revealing their lack of true knowledge.

His political philosophy invites reflection on contemporary democratic practices. In an age where information is abundant yet often unvetted, Socrates' emphasis on wisdom and informed decision-making is increasingly relevant. His vision of a governance led by the knowledgeable challenges modern societies to reconsider the principles of justice and the qualifications of those in positions of power.

The trial and execution of Socrates are among the most pivotal events in the history of Western philosophy. Charged with corrupting the youth and impiety, Socrates' defense, as recounted in Plato's "Apology," articulates a profound commitment to philosophical inquiry even in the face of death. His willingness to die for his principles rather than conform to societal pressures underscores the profound ethical integrity at the heart of his philosophy.

Socrates' unwavering commitment to the pursuit of truth and his method of dialectical inquiry have left an indelible mark on the intellectual landscape. His methods of questioning and the emphasis on self-examination have permeated various domains of human thought, encouraging a tradition of skepticism and critical thinking that remains at the core of philosophical practice today.

Moreover, his work has profound implications for contemporary thought and education, emphasizing the necessity of questioning and reflective dialogue in the pursuit of knowledge and ethical living. As we continue to navigate a world characterized by rapid technological change and complex moral dilemmas, the Socratic legacy serves as a beacon for those who seek to understand not just the world around them but also their own beliefs and actions.

Socrates not only transformed Western philosophy but also offered a way of living that is deeply relevant in today's world. His insistence on the examined life challenges individuals to engage critically with their own times and societies. His intellectual legacy, therefore, is not just in his specific philosophical doctrines but in his method of inquiry and his unwavering commitment to truth and virtue, resonating through ages as a fundamental call to philosophical and ethical engagement.

Now, keeping Socratic philosophers in mind, let's explore several pressing contemporary issues: political polarization, the environmental crisis, and the rise of technology in shaping human behavior.

## Political Polarization

Socrates, who famously engaged in discussions with Athenians from all walks of life, would likely be troubled by the current state of political polarization. His dialectical method was designed to bridge differences and encourage a shared pursuit of truth, rather than entrenching divisions. Socrates might approach this issue by initiating dialogues that probe the underlying beliefs and assumptions driving polarization. For instance, he would question individuals on all sides of the political spectrum, challenging them to define justice, the good life, and the role of government. Through his method of elenchus (refutation), he would expose contradictions in their views and guide them towards more coherent and reflective positions. In doing so, Socrates would emphasize the importance of seeing one's political opponents as partners in a shared quest for truth and the common good, rather than adversaries to be defeated.

## Environmental Crisis

Socrates would likely focus on the ethical implications of human actions affecting the planet. He would question the society's values around consumption and growth, asking whether these align with a virtuous life. Socrates would probe individuals to consider what it means to live in accordance with nature, an idea he valued, though more in an ethical than an ecological sense. Through a Socratic dialogue, he might lead people to see that excessive consumption and disregard for the natural world are inconsistent with the virtues of temperance and justice. He would encourage a reflection on how one's lifestyle choices reflect one's values and whether these choices contribute to a harmonious society and world. The goal would be to foster a sense of personal responsibility and encourage actions that align with the health of the planet, viewed as a common good for all humanity.

## Rise of Technology

The rise of technology, particularly its role in shaping human behavior and decision-making, presents a complex challenge that Socrates would find fascinating. He would be particularly interested in the ethical implications of technologies like social media, artificial intelligence, and surveillance systems. Socrates would question whether these technologies enhance or diminish true knowledge and virtue. For example, he might ask if the convenience of information technology leads to genuine understanding or merely a superficial accumulation of facts. Does social media promote real friendships, a key component of a good life according to him, or does it develop connections that are shallow and devoid of ethical substance? Through his questioning, Socrates would urge individuals to critically assess how technology impacts their lives and to consider how it can be used to truly enhance the well-being of the individual and the community, rather than manipulate or control behavior.

Through a Socratic critique of these contemporary issues, it becomes clear that many of the challenges we face today could benefit from a deeper philosophical inquiry into the values that underpin our choices and actions. Socrates' approach teaches us that by engaging in thoughtful dialogue, examining our lives and assumptions, and striving for ethical consistency, we can hope to address the complexities of our world more effectively. His philosophy does not provide easy answers but offers a method and a mindset that can lead to greater wisdom and a more virtuous, fulfilling life.

## ii. Plato (427 BCE - 347 BCE)

Plato, the distinguished student of Socrates and the founder of the Academy in Athens, is a cornerstone in the architecture of Western philosophy. His dialogues span the gamut of philosophical inquiry (ethics, politics, metaphysics, and epistemology) and have left an indelible mark on the intellectual tradition, influencing thinkers across millennia. Plato's philosophical journey was both a continuation and an expansion of Socratic thought, extending its reach into new realms of abstract and systemic thinking that have become foundational in Western intellectual history.

Born into an aristocratic Athenian family circa 427 BCE, Plato was initially poised for a career in politics. However, the pivotal execution of Socrates in 399 BCE, which Plato witnessed, redirected his life's trajectory towards philosophy. This event deeply affected him, crystallizing his distrust of Athenian democracy and shaping his philosophical convictions. In 387 BCE, he founded the Academy, which became the intellectual nexus of the Greek world and laid the groundwork for the modern university. His travels to places like Egypt, Italy, and Sicily expanded his perspective and enriched his philosophical dialogues.

Plato's works, predominantly dialogues with Socrates often cast as the protagonist, serve as complex layers of pedagogy, philosophy, and literature. Through these dialogues, Plato not only explores philosophical concepts but also models the process of dialectical thinking. One of his most profound contributions is the Theory of Forms, which posits that beyond our empirical reality lies a realm of abstract Forms or Ideas that represent the true essence of all things. This metaphysical realm, containing the perfect and eternal Forms, stands in contrast to the transient objects of our sensory world.

In "The Republic," Plato describes his vision of an ideal state ruled by philosopher-kings, guardians endowed with knowledge of the Forms, especially the Form of the Good. This ideal state, while criticized for its rigid class structure and apparent authoritarian leanings, underscores Plato's deep engagement with the conditions necessary for achieving justice. His political theory is intricately linked to his metaphysical views, as the philosopher-king's insight into the Forms enables just and enlightened governance.

Plato's reflections on democracy, presented through various regimes discussed in "The Republic" and "Laws," offer a nuanced examination of governance that resonates with contemporary debates on the nature and challenges of democratic systems. His skepticism towards pure democracy stems from a concern over the lack of philosophical wisdom among the masses, an idea that invites reflection on the role of education and moral development in contemporary political structures.

Central to Plato's metaphysical landscape is the Theory of Forms. He argues that the physical world is merely a shadow of the more real, unchanging world of Forms. The Form of the Good, the highest of these Forms, not only illuminates the existence of all other Forms but also represents the ultimate object of knowledge. This theory addresses classical problems of permanence and change and provides a foundation for Plato's ethical and political ideals by rooting concepts like justice, beauty, and equality in a timeless metaphysical reality.

Plato's impact on philosophy and Western culture cannot be overstated. His Academy nurtured future thinkers, including Aristotle, and his ideas became integral to Christian theology, medieval scholasticism, Renaissance humanism, and the Enlightenment. His work continues to inspire contemporary philosophical debate, particularly in the realms of ethics, political theory, and metaphysics.

Plato's exploration of ideal forms and rational inquiry also deeply informs modern dialogues about reality and perception, such as those explored in contemporary philosophical works that dissect the nature of knowledge, reality, and freewill. His allegory of the cave, for instance, serves as a potent metaphor for enlightenment and the pursuit of truth, reflecting the ongoing philosophical quest to understand the essence of human cognition and the nature of the world.

Through his dialogues, Plato invites us into a reflective space where we are encouraged to question our beliefs and assumptions. This process of examination and debate is crucial for navigating the complexities of modern existence and underscores the timeless relevance of Platonic philosophy. Plato's legacy, thus, is not only in the specific doctrines he espoused but also in his method of inquiry and his commitment to the philosophical examination of life. His enduring wisdom continues to offer insights into the pursuit of truth, beauty, justice, and the good life, shaping the intellectual contours of the contemporary world.

Just like before, let's look at some contemporary issues in light of Platonic philosophies:

## Political Polarization

Plato's critique of democracy in his work "The Republic" provides a foundation for understanding his likely view on political polarization. He was wary of democracy because it allows people, who might be swayed by persuasive rhetoric rather than truth, to make important decisions. This skepticism towards the masses' ability to govern wisely seems prescient in today's world of soundbite-driven politics and superficial media engagements. Plato might see political polarization as a symptom of a deeper problem: the lack of philosophical wisdom in public discourse and governance. He advocated for rulers who are philosopher-kings, individuals who understand the forms of justice, the good, and truth, and who could guide the polis away from factionalism toward a unified pursuit of the common good. In a modern context, Plato would likely argue for a greater emphasis on education that not only informs but also forms citizens capable of discerning the truth and engaging in reasoned dialogue, thereby reducing polarization.

## Environmental Crisis

Plato's understanding of the world as a reflection of more perfect forms would deeply color his perception of the environmental crisis. He believed that everything in the physical world strives to imitate its ideal form; thus, the degradation of the environment could be seen as a deviation from its ideal state of harmony and balance. From Plato's perspective, this crisis would signal a misalignment between human actions and the form of the Good, where the Good dictates a harmonious existence that respects the natural order. Plato would likely argue that the environmental crisis is a moral and ethical failure, a result of societies prioritizing material gain and short-term benefits over the long-term health of the planet, which aligns with the form of the Good. He would advocate for a philosophical reorientation towards values that promote sustainability, suggesting that leaders and citizens alike must understand and embody these ideals to resolve the crisis effectively.

## Rise of Technology

Plato's suspicion of the arts and sensory experiences as misleading could extend to a critique of technology, particularly digital media and its capacity to distort reality. In "The Republic," Plato uses the allegory of the cave to illustrate how humans can be deceived by appearances. Applied to modern technology, Plato might argue that digital environments, like social media platforms, create shadows of reality that can mislead and misinform, trapping users in a cave of illusions rather than enlightening them with truth. However, Plato also might see the potential for technology to aid in the pursuit of knowledge if it can be aligned with the true, the good, and the beautiful. For example, he might appreciate how technology can provide access to vast amounts of information and educational opportunities, but he would insist that this technology be used in ways that genuinely enhance understanding and lead people closer to the forms of truth and goodness.

From a Platonic perspective, contemporary societal issues often stem from a failure to align with the forms of truth, justice, and the good. To address issues like political polarization, environmental degradation, and the challenges posed by technology, Plato would advocate for a return to philosophical wisdom, both in leadership and in the general populace. He would see the need for societies to cultivate virtues that align with the ideal forms, promoting a more just, enlightened, and harmonious world. In this way, Plato's philosophy not only critiques modern issues but also provides a timeless framework for improving human societies by striving toward the ideals of the forms.

## iii. Aristotle (384 BCE - 322 BCE)

Aristotle, a towering figure in the landscape of Western philosophy, was a student of Plato and tutor to Alexander the Great. Born in Stagira in 384 BCE, his intellectual contributions span a broad spectrum of disciplines, including metaphysics, ethics, politics, biology, and aesthetics. Aristotle's profound influence shaped the foundations of Western thought and established systematic methodologies that underpinned the evolution of scientific and philosophical endeavors across the ages.

Aristotle's formative years at Plato's Academy in Athens were crucial; he spent two decades absorbing and later challenging Platonic philosophy. Unlike Plato, who elevated the realm of Forms as the true reality, Aristotle turned his attention to the empirical world. His focus was on understanding the observable universe and its underlying principles. After Plato's death, Aristotle's philosophical journey led him to Assos and the island of Lesbos, where he engaged in extensive biological research, and later to the Macedonian court to tutor Alexander the Great, an experience that enriched his perspectives on leadership and governance.

In 335 BCE, Aristotle founded the Lyceum in Athens, an institution where he developed his methodical approach to knowledge categorization, laying the groundwork for a comprehensive philosophical system. This period marked a significant expansion of his intellectual pursuits, characterized by the systematic collection and analysis of data, particularly in natural sciences.

Aristotle's empirical approach distinguished his philosophy from Plato's idealism. In his seminal work "Metaphysics," Aristotle introduced concepts such as substance, form, and matter, arguing that the essence of things lies in their empirical attributes and functionalities. This hylomorphic (matter-form) framework marked a departure from Platonic thought, grounding the understanding of existence in observable reality rather than abstract forms.

His theory of the "Four Causes" (material, formal, efficient, and final causes) offered a robust explanatory framework that spanned across disciplines, explaining both change and the nature of existence. This approach not only enriched the philosophical discourse but also laid foundational principles for the future development of the natural sciences.

In "Nicomachean Ethics," Aristotle articulated a comprehensive virtue ethics framework, centered around the concept of eudaimonia (flourishing or happiness). He posited that true happiness is achieved through virtuous activity aligned with reason, rather than through the pursuit of wealth or honor. Virtue, according to Aristotle, is about finding the mean between extremes, a balance that is cultivated through habituation and reflective choice, indicating a pragmatic approach to ethics focused on personal development and moral education.

Aristotle's "Politics" is a detailed examination of the polis (city-state), which he viewed as the pinnacle of human communal life. Contrary to Plato's idealistic schema, Aristotle endorsed a mixed constitution that incorporated elements of monarchy, aristocracy, and democracy, emphasizing the role of the middle class in maintaining societal equilibrium and advocating for governance that serves the common good of all citizens.

Aristotle's extensive work in biology and his meticulous classification systems were revolutionary. His observations in "History of Animals" and other biological texts demonstrated a keen analytical acumen that prefigured later scientific methods. In the realm of logic, Aristotle's "Organon" introduced formal deductive reasoning, notably the syllogism, which became foundational to subsequent intellectual inquiry.

His influence extended beyond the Hellenistic period, deeply affecting intellectual developments in the Roman Empire, the Islamic Golden Age, and medieval Europe. During the Renaissance, Aristotle's works were integral to university curricula, significantly shaping the discourse of Scholasticism and later Enlightenment thought. His methodologies and analytical frameworks continue to inform contemporary philosophical debates, particularly in the fields of ethics, political theory, metaphysics, and the philosophy of science.

Aristotle's empirical methods and commitment to systematic inquiry laid the intellectual groundwork for the Scientific Revolution and have continued to inspire discussions on the nature of knowledge, reality, and ethical conduct. His legacy is a testament to the enduring power of observation and reason in the quest to understand and articulate the complexities of the natural and human worlds. Through his comprehensive body of work, Aristotle has equipped generations with the intellectual tools necessary for critical thinking and reasoned analysis, underscoring his pivotal role in shaping the trajectory of Western intellectual history.

Now we look at political polarization, environmental degradation, and the rise of technology from an Aristotelian perspective:

## Political Polarization

Aristotle's political philosophy, as articulated in his work "Politics," emphasizes the role of the polis (city-state) in facilitating the good life for its citizens. He believed that the polis should cultivate virtue and enable its citizens to live fulfilling lives. In the context of political polarization, Aristotle would likely focus on the need for civic virtue and the cultivation of a political community that seeks the common good rather than partisan interests. Aristotle would probably diagnose modern political polarization as a failure of phronesis, or practical wisdom, among both leaders and citizens. Practical wisdom in politics involves finding the right means to achieve the common good and requires an understanding of how to balance competing interests and opinions in a way that is just and conducive to the well-being of the community. He might suggest that to mitigate polarization, societies need to develop a political culture that prioritizes dialogue, mutual respect, and an understanding that the ultimate goal of politics is not victory over opponents but the flourishing of the community.

## Environmental Crisis

Aristotle's understanding of nature and his teleological view of the world, that everything has a purpose or end (telos), provide a unique perspective on environmental issues. He believed that everything in nature has an inherent purpose, and the highest human good involves living in accordance with reason, which aligns with the natural order. From an Aristotelian standpoint, the environmental crisis could be seen as a manifestation of humanity's failure to recognize and respect the natural purposes inherent in the world. This crisis results from excessive and irrational exploitation of natural resources, contrary to the virtue of temperance, which dictates moderation and balance. Aristotle would advocate for a more virtuous approach to environmental stewardship, one that respects the natural purposes of the earth's ecosystems and seeks to maintain balance and sustainability.

## Rise of Technology

Aristotle's philosophy also provides a valuable perspective on the rise of technology, especially concerning human well-being and ethical considerations. While Aristotle did not confront technology in the modern sense, his emphasis on the purpose of human life and the role of tools in achieving human ends can be applied to this issue. He might view modern technology as a means that should enhance human flourishing and not detract from it. Technology, in the Aristotelian view, ought to serve as an instrument that helps individuals achieve their telos, which is rational activity in accordance with virtue. However, if technology leads to alienation, diminishes face-to-face interactions, or encourages behaviors that are not aligned with human flourishing, then it is not serving its proper function.

Aristotle would likely have mixed feelings about technologies like social media. On one hand, if used to enhance knowledge and foster meaningful community connections, it aligns with human purposes. On the other hand, if it leads to distraction, superficial relationships, or ethical lapses (such as privacy violations or misinformation), it would be considered harmful to human flourishing.

From an Aristotelian perspective, contemporary societal issues often stem from a misalignment between modern practices and the pursuit of the good life defined by reason and virtue. Addressing these issues requires a recalibration of individual and collective goals towards those that truly enhance human flourishing. Whether discussing political life, environmental stewardship, or technological advancements, Aristotle would encourage a return to the fundamental questions about the purposes these aspects of life serve and how they contribute to the ultimate goal of living well. His approach underscores the importance of cultivating virtue, practical wisdom, and a keen awareness of the true ends of human activities.

# IV. The Sophists (~500 BCE to ~400 BCE)

The Sophists, itinerant educators and intellectuals of ancient Greece, emerged in the 5th century BCE as pivotal figures who revolutionized the traditional approaches to philosophy, ethics, rhetoric, and political thought. Known for their travels across Greece, they offered education to young aristocrats on various subjects, including virtue and the art of persuasion, and were among the first to charge for their teachings, thus valuing knowledge as a commodity. This practice, along with their often controversial teachings, stirred significant debate regarding the nature and value of knowledge and education.

Central to Sophistic philosophy was a form of moral and epistemological relativism, eloquently summarized by Protagoras's declaration, "Man is the measure of all things." This assertion implies that truth and morality are not universal absolutes but are subjective, contingent upon individual perceptions and experiences. This relativistic stance not only challenged the prevailing notions of objective truth upheld by their predecessors but also laid the groundwork for future philosophical discourses that questioned the absolutes of truth and ethics.

The Sophists were master rhetoricians, known for their capacity to make weaker arguments appear stronger, enhancing their appeal to the aristocracy, who sought political influence in democratic assemblies. However, this adept use of rhetoric was not universally admired; critics like Plato accused the Sophists of undermining the moral and judicial foundations of the city-state by favoring persuasive success over factual or ethical accuracy. This criticism highlights a profound tension in classical Greek philosophy regarding the purpose and ethical dimensions of rhetorical skill.

In their political and legal theories, the Sophists advocated for a critical reassessment of existing laws and norms. They distinguished between natural laws (physis), which are immutable and universal, and conventional laws (nomos), which are human constructs and subject to change. This perspective encouraged progressive thinking about law and governance, suggesting that legal systems should evolve to align more closely with reason and natural justice. This progressive stance not only incited debates about the nature and source of laws but also encouraged a more dynamic interaction between societal norms and philosophical inquiry.

Despite their significant contributions, the Sophists faced substantial criticism, particularly from figures like Socrates and his student Plato. Socrates challenged the Sophistic assertion that virtue could be taught as a mere skill, advocating instead for an understanding of virtue rooted in universal truths rather than the relativistic approach favored by the Sophists. Plato, through his dialogues, often cast the Sophists as philosophical adversaries who engaged in ethical and intellectual malpractices, corrupting the youth with relativism and skepticism.

The Sophistic focus on the subjective nature of truth and their methodological innovations in rhetoric had enduring impacts on the intellectual landscape of Greece, influencing the evolution of democratic discourse and educational practices. Their ideas resonate in modern philosophical debates, particularly within postmodern thought, which similarly challenges the stability of meaning and the possibility of objective knowledge. The legacy of the Sophists underscores the importance of continual critical engagement with philosophical, ethical, and social norms, reflecting the complexities of human experience and the perennial tension between skepticism and certainty.

Overall, the Sophists not only challenged the philosophical status quo of their time but also fostered a critical dialogue that continues to influence contemporary thought. Their exploration of rhetoric, law, and morality remains a testament to the dynamic interplay between philosophical inquiry and societal development, reminding us of the lasting value of questioning prevailing truths and the multifaceted nature of knowledge and justice in human societies. Let's explore how they might view political polarization, environmental issues, and the rise of technology.

## Political Polarization

Sophists would likely view political polarization as a fertile ground for the exercise of rhetoric and persuasion, skills they highly valued and taught. Given their relativistic view of truth, where what is "true" can often depend on the persuasiveness of arguments, Sophists might approach polarization not as a problem to be solved through finding objective truths but as a reality to be navigated through effective communication and argumentation. In dealing with political polarization, Sophists would likely emphasize the importance of rhetoric in shaping public opinion and political outcomes. They might advocate for more skillful persuasion in political discourse, encouraging politicians and public figures to better understand and appeal to different perspectives. The Sophistic approach would focus on adapting arguments to audiences to achieve practical outcomes, rather than seeking consensus on what is universally true or just.

## Environmental Crisis

When addressing environmental issues, Sophists might focus on the rhetoric surrounding environmental conservation and climate change rather than the scientific or ethical aspects. They would recognize the power of persuasive communication in shaping public and political responses to environmental challenges. A Sophist today might argue that effective environmental action depends on the ability to convincingly articulate the consequences of inaction and the benefits of sustainable practices. Furthermore, Sophists might question the prevailing narratives about the environment from various angles, demonstrating how different presentations of facts can lead to different public responses. They would likely explore how definitions of terms like "sustainability" and "conservation" are constructed and used in public discourse, analyzing these terms for their rhetorical effectiveness rather than their truth content.

## Rise of Technology

The Sophists' approach to the rise of technology would likely focus on the persuasive potential of digital media and the ethical implications of such technologies in shaping human thought and behavior. They would be interested in how arguments are framed in digital platforms, how consensus is formed online, and how technology can be used to persuade and manipulate public opinion. Sophists would probably be critical of any claims about technology that purport to be absolute truths, instead highlighting how technology itself is a tool that can be used for various ends, depending on how it is presented and argued for in public and private spheres. They might also focus on teaching individuals how to effectively use digital rhetoric to their advantage, emphasizing the development of critical thinking skills to navigate the complex information landscape that technology creates.

From a Sophist perspective, the complexities of these modern issues are best approached through the lens of effective rhetoric and the understanding that truth is often a matter of perception shaped by persuasive argument. The Sophists would encourage a pragmatic approach to these issues, where success is measured by the ability to achieve desired outcomes through skillful persuasion and adaptability in the face of differing opinions and facts. They would stress the importance of understanding how arguments are constructed and deconstructed, advocating for a sophisticated command of language and presentation as essential tools in any endeavor, whether political, environmental, or technological.

# V. Diogenes and the Cynics (~400 BCE to ~320 BCE)

Diogenes of Sinope, the emblematic figure of the Cynic movement, personified a philosophy that starkly contrasts with many of today's societal norms, particularly consumerism. His ascetic lifestyle, which included living minimally in a simple tub and possessing only basic necessities, underscored his commitment to a life guided by nature and virtue, free from the trappings of wealth and social status.

The Cynics, often derided for their "dog-like" approach to life, chose a path of deliberate simplicity and rigorous self-sufficiency. They questioned the prevailing Greek ethos that equated success with accumulation and prestige, positing instead that true good arises solely from virtue and living in natural harmony. This perspective not only challenged the materialistic values of their time but also offered a precursor to modern minimalism, which similarly emphasizes paring life down to the essentials and finding fulfillment beyond material wealth.

The contrast between Cynic philosophy and contemporary consumerism is profound. Consumerism often encourages the acquisition of goods and a lifestyle of excess as pathways to happiness, inherently suggesting that value and success are externally defined. Diogenes and his followers would have viewed such pursuits as distractions from true contentment and personal autonomy. They advocated for a return to simplicity, arguing that by shedding unnecessary desires and possessions, one could achieve a higher state of freedom and happiness—themes that resonate strongly with today's minimalist movements.

However, while minimalism in contemporary settings shares similarities with Cynic philosophy in its critique of material excess, it differs in its approach and rationale. Modern minimalism often focuses on decluttering physical spaces and simplifying lifestyle choices to reduce stress and increase efficiency, rather than pursuing these practices as inherently virtuous or as essential parts of ethical living. In this sense, minimalism can be seen as compatible with consumerism when it becomes another style or trend that markets products designed to help one "declutter."

In contrast, the Cynic's adoption of minimalism was not about aesthetic or superficial simplicity but was deeply entwined with their ethical views on the corruption caused by luxury and artificial needs. Their lifestyle was a form of philosophical protest against the societal norms that equated happiness with external acquisition and status. This more radical stance questions not only the pursuit of material goods but the very foundations of societal values and norms that define success and happiness.

Furthermore, the Cynic practice of parrhesia, or fearless speech, highlights another dimension of their philosophy that is especially relevant today. In an age of political turmoil and misinformation, the Cynic commitment to speaking truth to power and challenging authority offers a robust framework for advocating social and ethical integrity. This aspect of Cynic philosophy extends beyond personal lifestyle choices to engage with broader societal and political issues, reinforcing the idea that true freedom comes from ethical consistency and the courage to live authentically in the face of societal pressures.

Thus, Diogenes and the Cynics not only challenge us to reassess our relationship with material possessions but also invite a more profound reflection on how societal norms influence our understanding of success and happiness. Their legacy encourages a critical examination of consumer culture and promotes a life of authenticity and ethical integrity, providing a compelling philosophical foundation for those seeking to navigate the complexities of modern life in a principled and meaningful way.

## Political Polarization

Diogenes and the Cynics would likely view modern political polarization with a mix of disdain and indifference, seeing it as a manifestation of misplaced priorities and a misunderstanding of what truly matters in life. They might argue that the intense focus on political identity and partisan conflict is a distraction from the pursuit of self-sufficiency and personal virtue. In their view, true independence comes from freeing oneself from societal influences and the passions that politics so often stirs. Diogenes, in particular, might respond to political debates and strife by demonstrating absurdity or mocking the pretensions of political leaders, much as he did in ancient Athens. His approach would not be to provide a solution within the political framework but to question the framework itself, urging a return to simpler, more natural ways of living that are less dependent on complex political structures.

## Environmental Crisis

The environmental crisis would likely resonate more with Cynic philosophy, as it aligns with their emphasis on living in accordance with nature. Diogenes and his followers would harshly criticize modern societies for their estrangement from natural living and their excessive consumption, which they would see as the root causes of environmental degradation. The Cynic response to the environmental crisis would be radical and uncompromising. They would advocate for a drastic simplification of human life, reducing consumption to what is necessary and natural, thus minimizing human impact on the environment. This perspective challenges the very foundations of modern consumer society, advocating for a form of environmentalism that is not about managing resources better but about transforming the way humans view and value the natural world.

## Rise of Technology

Diogenes and the Cynics would likely have a critical view of the rise of technology, particularly concerning its role in shaping human relationships and societal values. They would criticize the way technology often reinforces the pursuit of pleasures and conveniences that they deem unnatural and unnecessary. In their view, technology distracts people from the pursuit of virtue and encourages a dependence on external tools rather than on one's own internal resources. The Cynics would be particularly skeptical of social media and other forms of digital communication, which they might see as poor substitutes for genuine, face-to-face human interaction. They would critique these technologies for fostering superficial relationships and for being tools that promote vanity, fame, and the desire for external validation, all of which are antithetical to Cynic values.

Through the lens of Diogenes and the Cynics, contemporary issues are critiqued not just for their surface-level problems but for the deeper philosophical and ethical misalignments they reveal about modern society. Their philosophy calls for a radical reevaluation of societal values, urging a return to simpler, more natural ways of living that emphasize personal virtue and independence from societal expectations. This perspective challenges us to reconsider what we value and why, pushing for a form of ethical radicalism that seeks to upend conventional life in the pursuit of what is natural and true.

# VI. Zeno and the Stoics (336 BCE - 265 BCE)

Zeno of Citium, a pivotal figure in the annals of philosophy, founded Stoicism in the early 3rd century BCE, a doctrine that has shaped countless lives and ideologies across millennia. Stoicism, as Zeno conceived it, was a rigorous synthesis of ethical vigor and metaphysical inquiry, drawing from his encounters with Socratic dialogues and the ascetic teachings of the Cynic philosopher Crates of Thebes. From these influences, Zeno developed a systematic philosophy that emphasized virtue, reason, and resilience as the cornerstones of a good life.

After being shipwrecked and stranded in Athens, Zeno's intellectual journey led him to the Stoa Poikile (Painted Porch), where he and his disciples discussed their ideas, hence the name Stoicism. The philosophy asserts that living in harmony with nature and its inherent rational order, or logos, leads to true flourishing, or eudaimonia. This rational order, according to the Stoics, is ubiquitous, governing the cosmos and human affairs alike, and thus, human happiness is achieved through recognizing and adhering to this natural logic.

Central to Stoic thought is the belief that virtue is the only true good and is sufficient for happiness. This idea diverges markedly from other philosophical doctrines that also value external goods such as wealth or reputation. In Stoic ethics, external factors are deemed 'indifferents', they do not inherently affect one's moral state and can be either beneficial or detrimental depending on one's internal use of them. The Stoic ideal is not to dismiss such externals but to engage with them virtuously, maintaining emotional equanimity regardless of life's vicissitudes.

The emphasis Stoicism places on inner tranquility and resilience is perhaps what makes it most compelling. Stoic teachings advocate that individuals can maintain peace by focusing on what they can control—their judgments, impulses, and actions, while accepting those things beyond their control. This philosophy was vividly practiced by figures such as Epictetus, who in his "Enchiridion," distilled the essence of Stoic resilience: distinguishing between our control over internal states and surrender to external circumstances.

This Stoic dichotomy between the controllable and uncontrollable has deeply influenced not only personal mindsets but also broad societal norms, particularly through the adoption by key historical figures like Seneca and Marcus Aurelius. Seneca's writings offer guidance on navigating ethical dilemmas in everyday life, whereas Marcus Aurelius' "Meditations" provide a personal testament to living Stoically under the pressures of imperial governance.

Beyond its ancient roots, Stoicism has permeated various aspects of modern life, influencing Christian moral teachings, Enlightenment philosophy, and even contemporary therapeutic practices such as cognitive-behavioral therapy. This modern psychotherapeutic approach echoes Stoic principles by encouraging individuals to challenge irrational beliefs and foster emotional well-being through reasoned thought.

In contemporary society, Stoicism has seen a resurgence, appealing to those seeking practical strategies for coping with the challenges of modern life. Its pragmatic focus on virtue, community, and rationality offers a resilient framework for personal development and social engagement. Stoic practices such as mindfulness, gratitude, and reflective contemplation are increasingly integrated into everyday wellness routines, highlighting the philosophy's enduring relevance. Writers like Massimo Pigliucci and Donald Robertson have played pivotal roles in translating Stoic philosophy for a modern audience, demonstrating how its ancient wisdom can provide profound insights into living ethically, maintaining emotional strength, and finding meaning in today's world. Through their works and the broader Stoic revival, the teachings of Zeno and his followers continue to inspire a quest for a fulfilled life guided by reason and moral integrity, proving the timeless appeal of Stoic philosophy.

## Political Polarization

The Stoics would approach the issue of political polarization with a focus on the virtues of wisdom and justice, emphasizing the need for rational discourse and cooperative behavior. Zeno, who believed in the idea of a cosmopolitan society where all individuals are citizens of the world, would advocate for seeing beyond local and national divisions to the shared rationality and humanity of all people. Stoicism teaches that external differences are indifferents, things that do not truly contribute to the good life defined by virtue. Stoic philosophy would encourage individuals engaged in political debates to focus on what can be controlled, their own responses and behaviors. Stoics would counsel against allowing external events to disturb one's inner peace and would recommend engaging in politics in a manner that is consistent with reason and the common good, rather than partisan victory.

## Environmental Crisis

Stoicism's commitment to living in accordance with nature provides a clear framework for addressing environmental issues. The Stoics would view the environmental crisis as a significant disruption to the natural order, which affects all living beings. Therefore, they would argue for a responsible and rational response to environmental degradation, emphasizing our duty as rational beings to protect and preserve the natural world for future generations. Zeno and his followers would likely see the environmental crisis as a call to practice the virtue of temperance, moderating our desires and consumption to live more sustainably. They would also see it as an opportunity to exercise the virtue of courage, facing the challenges of environmental action head-on, and justice, ensuring that we leave a habitable world for others.

## Rise of Technology

When it comes to the rise of technology, the Stoics would focus on the ways technology can be used to support or hinder virtuous living. They would not be inherently opposed to technology, as Stoicism does not reject external things but instead teaches that their value depends on their use. Technology that enhances our ability to live according to virtue, improves our understanding of the world, and helps us connect meaningfully with others could be viewed positively. However, Zeno and his followers would caution against becoming dependent on technology or allowing it to distract us from the pursuit of virtue. They would be particularly critical of ways that technology might foster negative emotions, such as envy or anger, or lead to moral disengagement. Instead, they would advocate using technology in ways that are aligned with Stoic principles, enhancing self-control, rationality, and community building.

Zeno and the Stoics provide a perspective that is deeply relevant to addressing contemporary issues. By focusing on the development of personal virtue and the importance of rational action, Stoicism offers tools for individuals to navigate the complexities of modern life. Stoicism teaches that maintaining inner tranquility and focusing on what one can control leads to more effective and ethical engagement with the world. This philosophy encourages a balanced and thoughtful approach to modern problems, emphasizing resilience, community responsibility, and the pursuit of a virtuous life.

## VII. Epicurus and the Epicureans (341 BCE - 270 BCE)

Epicurus, born in Samos in 341 BCE and later establishing his school, the Garden, in Athens, profoundly influenced the Hellenistic period's philosophical landscape. His philosophy, centered on the pursuit of happiness through the elimination of pain, offered a counter-narrative to the Stoic and Cynic philosophies of his time. Epicureanism, with its hedonistic ethics, emphasis on friendship, and counsel for a life removed from political tumult, provides a rich vein of thought that resonates with contemporary quests for well-being and understanding the nature of happiness.

At the heart of Epicurean philosophy is the principle that pleasure (hedone) is the highest good and the foundation of a happy life. However, Epicurus's conception of pleasure was far from the indulgence typically associated with hedonism. Instead, he advocated for ataraxia, tranquility of the soul and absence of bodily pain, as the highest form of pleasure. Epicurus posited that true happiness comes from simple pleasures, the cultivation of virtuous friendships, and the philosophical life. Epicurus's famous tetrapharmakos, or four-part cure, encapsulates his teachings: don't fear the gods; don't worry about death; what is good is easy to obtain; what is terrible is easy to endure. This succinct guide aimed to liberate individuals from the fears and desires that perturb the soul, offering a path to tranquility and happiness.

Contrary to popular misconceptions of Epicureanism as self-indulgent, Epicurus placed great value on friendship and community as essential components of a happy life. He argued that friendship offers security, mutual support, and the opportunity to practice virtues for the sake of one's friends, rather than for abstract moral principles. The Epicurean community, or Garden, served as a model for a life shared in pursuit of mutual happiness and understanding, emphasizing the role of social bonds in the attainment of tranquility.

Epicurus's natural philosophy posited that the universe is composed of atoms and void, governed by natural laws rather than divine intervention. This materialistic view of the world aimed to dispel fears of divine wrath and the afterlife, advocating for a serene acceptance of nature's workings. Epicurus's denial of an afterlife, encapsulated in his assertion that "death is nothing to us," sought to remove the fear of death, encouraging followers to focus on living a fulfilling life in the present. Epicurean ethics teaches the discernment of desires into three categories: natural and necessary (such as food and shelter), natural but not necessary (such as rich foods), and neither natural nor necessary (such as fame). Epicurus argued that true happiness comes from satisfying the first category of desires, while the pursuit of unnecessary desires leads to pain and disturbance. This pragmatic approach to ethics, focusing on the tangible benefits of virtuous living, offers a practical guide to happiness that remains relevant in contemporary discussions on well-being and contentment.

Epicurean philosophy deeply influenced Roman thinkers like Lucretius, whose poem "De Rerum Natura" offers a comprehensive exposition of Epicurean cosmology and ethics. Despite being marginalized in the medieval period, Epicureanism was rediscovered during the Renaissance, contributing to the development of modern scientific thought and secular ethics. In contemporary times, the principles of Epicureanism have found resonance in movements advocating for simplicity, mindfulness, and environmental sustainability. Philosophers like Michel Onfray have championed a neo-Epicurean lifestyle, arguing for the relevance of Epicurean ethics in addressing the challenges of consumerism and the search for meaning in a post-religious world.

Epicurus and the Epicureans provide a compelling vision of a life well-lived, characterized by the pursuit of simple pleasures, the cultivation of friendships, and the application of reason to overcome fear and superstition. Their philosophy, far from advocating hedonistic indulgence, offers a disciplined approach to happiness that emphasizes the importance of ethical reflection, community, and the understanding of nature. Epicureanism challenges us to reconsider our values and aspirations, advocating for a life of moderation, contemplation, and mutual care, principles that continue to offer guidance in the quest for a fulfilling and virtuous life.

## Political Polarization

Epicurus generally advised against involvement in politics, viewing it as a source of unnecessary disturbance that could disrupt one's peace of mind. He recommended leading a quiet life, where interactions and engagements are chosen based on how they affect one's tranquility. In the context of modern political polarization, Epicurus would likely advise individuals to focus on cultivating personal happiness and virtue in a manner that minimizes conflict and distress. Epicureans might view political polarization as a disruption that stems from unnecessary desires for power and status, which are contrary to the pursuit of a tranquil life. Instead of engaging in heated political debates, Epicureans would advocate for withdrawal from contentious public discourse, suggesting that individuals focus on building supportive communities that foster mutual respect and understanding.

## Environmental Crisis

While Epicurus did not specifically address environmental issues, his philosophy places a high value on living in harmony with nature as a means to achieve tranquility. The environmental crisis could be seen as a significant threat to peaceful living, not only because of the physical dangers it poses but also due to the psychological stress associated with concerns about the future of the planet. Epicureans would likely advocate for practical measures that individuals can take to reduce their impact on the environment, promoting a lifestyle that aligns with Epicurean simplicity and self-sufficiency. By focusing on natural and necessary desires, those that genuinely contribute to health and well-being, and eliminating unnecessary consumption, Epicureans would argue that one can live a more environmentally conscious life that is also more conducive to achieving personal peace.

## Rise of Technology

The Epicurean philosophy might have a nuanced view of the rise of technology, recognizing both its potential benefits and its risks to tranquility. On one hand, technology can enhance our ability to meet basic needs more efficiently, reduce physical pain, and even help maintain social connections. These aspects would be seen positively by Epicureans, as they can contribute to aponia and social pleasure, which are important for happiness. On the other hand, Epicurus would caution against the ways technology can lead to psychological disturbances, such as anxiety, envy, and dissatisfaction, stemming from constant connectivity and the bombardment of information. The Epicurean approach would advocate for a balanced use of technology, emphasizing moderation and mindfulness to ensure that technological engagement does not detract from tranquility and the enjoyment of simple pleasures.

Epicurus and the Epicureans provide a perspective focused on achieving personal tranquility and happiness through simple living, wise choices, and the cultivation of friendships. In addressing modern issues like political polarization, environmental crises, and the proliferation of technology, Epicureanism offers valuable insights into how to navigate these challenges in ways that maintain peace of mind. By prioritizing what is natural and necessary, avoiding unnecessary desires, and fostering supportive social environments, Epicureanism remains a relevant and practical philosophy for contemporary life, guiding individuals in their quest for a tranquil and fulfilling existence.

## VIII. Pyrrho and the Skeptics (360 BCE to 270 BCE)

Pyrrho of Elis, who lived around 360-270 BCE, emerged as a central figure in the development of Skepticism, profoundly shaping this philosophical tradition with ideas that reverberate through centuries of Western thought. His travels to India, where he encountered Eastern philosophies during Alexander the Great's campaigns, significantly influenced his outlook and the philosophical tenets he would later develop in Greece. These experiences introduced him to concepts that underscored the limits of human knowledge and the value of mental peace, elements that deeply informed his skeptical approach.

The core of Pyrrhonian Skepticism is its advocacy for the suspension of judgment (epoché), proposing that since human senses and reason are inherently fallible, true certainty about the nature of reality remains elusive. For Pyrrho and his followers, this was not merely a theoretical stance but a practical methodology aimed at achieving tranquility (ataraxia). By disengaging from the pursuit of definitive truths and instead embracing a state of open inquiry, Skeptics sought to liberate themselves from the distress commonly associated with rigid dogmatic beliefs.

This suspension of judgment was seen not as an end in itself but as a means to attain a profound peace of mind. Pyrrho's philosophy suggested that equilibrium could be maintained by recognizing that for every argument, there exists a counterargument of equal plausibility. This idea promoted a life characterized by adaptability and open-mindedness, where peace is derived not from certainty but from an acceptance of perpetual uncertainty.

Sextus Empiricus, who later systematized Pyrrho's teachings, emphasized that this detachment from dogmatic belief was crucial in achieving mental peace, framing skepticism as a liberation from the tyranny of absolute thinking. This perspective was instrumental in shaping the Academic skepticism that would take root in Plato's Academy and influenced a wide array of philosophical discourse from the Hellenistic period to the Roman era and beyond.

The impact of Pyrrhonian Skepticism extended far into the intellectual currents of Europe, resonating with thinkers like Montaigne, Hume, and Kant, all of whom grappled with the boundaries of human reason and the pursuit of knowledge. These philosophers engaged with the skeptical tradition in various ways, often using it as a foundation to explore the criteria for knowledge and the reliability of human cognition.

In the modern world, characterized by an overload of information and a myriad of conflicting worldviews, Pyrrho's skeptical philosophy gains renewed relevance. It challenges the modern individual to embrace humility, question deeply held assumptions, and find contentment in the absence of absolute certainty. This approach, which values intellectual flexibility and continuous inquiry, offers a valuable perspective in navigating contemporary challenges, fostering a mindset that prioritizes peace and balanced living over the conquest of truth.

The enduring legacy of Pyrrho and the Skeptics not only enriches philosophical discourse but also offers practical insights into living ethically and peacefully in a complex world. Their teachings encourage a form of engagement with life that is dynamically responsive to changing circumstances and informed by a deep-seated humility about our capacities for knowledge. In this way, Skepticism not only contributes to ongoing debates in moral and political philosophy but also provides a framework for understanding and coping with the uncertainties inherent in human existence.

## Political Polarization

Pyrrho and the Skeptics would likely view political polarization as a result of dogmatic beliefs held too rigidly by individuals on all sides of the political spectrum. Skeptics argue that because our senses and rational capacities are fallible, certainty about political doctrines or ideologies is unachievable. As a result, they would recommend suspending judgment on these matters to avoid the disturbances that come from contentious political disputes. In dealing with political polarization, Skeptics would advocate for an approach that recognizes the limits of our knowledge and encourages a posture of open inquiry without committing to a fixed position. This could potentially reduce conflict, as it removes the usual grounds for contention, firm beliefs that one's own views are undeniably correct. Such a stance might promote a more cooperative and less adversarial political environment, where dialogue and understanding are prioritized over winning arguments.

## Environmental Crisis

Concerning the environmental crisis, Pyrrho and his followers might initially question the various claims about the causes and extents of environmental damage, not out of denial but as a methodological skepticism. They would challenge both the doom-laden narratives and the dismissive ones, pushing for a balanced view that acknowledges the limitations of our predictive powers and scientific certainties. However, given the potential for significant harm, Skeptics might adopt a practical stance that aligns with the principle of non-dogmatic living. While suspending judgment on absolute claims about the environment, they might still support pragmatic actions to mitigate risk and promote well-being. This approach resembles the precautionary principle in environmental science, acting in a way that is cautious and mindful of potential harms, thus maintaining tranquility in the face of uncertain threats.

## Rise of Technology

Skeptics would approach the rise of technology by questioning the underlying assumptions about its benefits and harms. They would neither wholly embrace nor entirely reject technological advancements; instead, they would encourage a continual examination of how technology influences human life and society. Pyrrho and the Skeptics might be particularly cautious about claims that technology unequivocally improves life or, conversely, that it inevitably leads to societal decay. Instead, they would advocate for an individual and collective examination of how technology is used and its actual impacts on human tranquility and well-being. This skeptical approach could lead to more thoughtful and less reactionary uses of technology, emphasizing mindful engagement over passive consumption.

Pyrrho and the Skeptics provide a philosophical framework that emphasizes doubt, inquiry, and the suspension of judgment as tools to navigate the complexities of modern life. By questioning certainties and maintaining a stance of open inquiry, Skepticism encourages a form of engagement with the world that is less about holding and defending positions and more about adapting to realities as they are understood in the moment. This can foster a more peaceful and less confrontational approach to contemporary issues, from political debates to environmental challenges and the integration of technology into daily life, ultimately allowing individuals to live with less disturbance amidst a rapidly changing world.

# Chapter 4: The Late Antiquity to the Medieval Period

The Greek Philosophical Era was followed by a period of significant intellectual, cultural, and historical developments across the late antiquity, the Middle Ages, and the early modern period. This era, often underestimated in its philosophical richness, served as a foundation for the preservation, transformation, and expansion of Greek philosophical insights, which later became integral to the Renaissance revival of classical antiquity. The main influencers during this intermediary period include a diverse array of thinkers from the realms of Christian, Islamic, and Jewish philosophy, each contributing to the preservation and reinterpretation of ancient wisdom.

Late antiquity marks the transition from classical to medieval thought, characterized by the integration of Greek philosophy into Christian theology. Figures like Augustine of Hippo and Boethius played pivotal roles in this process. Augustine's works, especially "Confessions" and "The City of God," blend Platonic and Christian thought, exploring the nature of God, the soul, and the ethical life within a Christian framework. Boethius, in "The Consolation of Philosophy," employs Platonic and Aristotelian concepts to discuss fate, free will, and happiness, bridging classical philosophy with Christian teachings.

The Islamic Golden Age, spanning the 8th to the 14th century, witnessed the translation of Greek philosophical works into Arabic, preserving them for future generations. Scholars like Al-Farabi, Avicenna (Ibn Sina), and Averroes (Ibn Rushd) not only safeguarded Greek philosophy but also expanded upon it, contributing original insights into metaphysics, logic, and ethics. Avicenna's "The Book of Healing" and Averroes' commentaries on Aristotle were particularly influential, introducing complex discussions on being, essence, and the rational soul.

Jewish philosophers like Moses Maimonides played a crucial role in this period with works like "Guide for the Perplexed," which harmonizes Aristotelian philosophy with Jewish theology to address the nature of God, the universe, and the path to intellectual and spiritual fulfillment. His work, deeply rooted in Greek thought and Jewish scripture, illustrates the intercultural dialogue that defined the intellectual landscape of the Middle Ages.

The Medieval period in Europe saw the rise of Scholasticism, a method of learning that sought to reconcile Christian theology with Aristotelian philosophy. Thinkers like Thomas Aquinas, Duns Scotus, and William of Ockham were instrumental in this synthesis. Aquinas, in his "Summa Theologica," integrates Aristotelian logic and metaphysics into Christian doctrine, arguing for the compatibility of faith and reason. The Scholastics' rigorous analytical approach & development of the university system laid the groundwork for the intellectual flourishing of the Renaissance.

The Renaissance was not only a rebirth of classical art and literature but also a period of significant philosophical inquiry deeply influenced by the works of these intermediary thinkers. The humanists of the Renaissance, inspired by the translations and commentaries of Islamic and Jewish scholars, rediscovered Greek and Roman texts, which led to a revival of Platonic and Aristotelian thought in a new cultural and intellectual context. This era saw the emergence of figures like Erasmus, who advocated for a return to the sources (ad fontes) and emphasized the value of classical education, and Marsilio Ficino, whose translations of Plato reinvigorated Platonic philosophy in the West.

## i. The Late Antiquity (~300 CE to ~800 CE)

Late Antiquity, a period that stretches from the 3rd to the 8th century CE, serves as a crucial bridge between the classical world of Greek and Roman philosophy and the intellectual ferment of the Middle Ages and Renaissance. This era is marked by profound transformations within the Roman Empire, the spread of Christianity and Islam, and significant cultural and philosophical exchanges. Amidst this backdrop of change, Late Antiquity witnessed the synthesis of classical philosophical traditions with emerging religious ideas, leading to new schools of thought that would profoundly influence the course of Western intellectual history.

One of the defining features of Late Antiquity is the integration of Hellenistic philosophical principles with Christian theology. Figures such as Augustine of Hippo stand out for their efforts to reconcile Platonic philosophy with Christian doctrine. **Augustine of Hippo** (354 - 430 CE) stands as a notable figure in this era, adjoining Christian doctrine with the rich aftermath of Platonic philosophy. His intellectual journey from a **Manichean critic** (*Manichaeism was a major world religion founded during the 3rd century BCE by Mani, an Iranian "Prophet," focused on unifying the world religions. It primarily prevailed during the Late Antiquity.*) of Christianity to a Bishop and Christian thinker underscores the era's interwebed ideas. In works like "Confessions," Augustine explores themes of sin, grace, and redemption, employing a deeply introspective narrative that reflects Platonic influences, particularly in his conceptualization of the immaterial world and the ascent of the soul towards God. His "City of God," written in the aftermath of Rome's sack, presents a vision of human history as a drama between the "City of God" and the "City of Man," using Neoplatonic ideas to articulate a Christian philosophy of history and eschatology. Augustine's integration of faith and reason laid foundational stones for the development of Western theology and philosophy, marking him as a pivotal figure in bridging classical and Christian thought.

Late Antiquity also saw the preservation of classical knowledge through the work of scholars like Boethius, who sought to translate and comment on the entire corpus of Aristotle's work and Plato's dialogues. **Anicius Manlius Severinus Boëthius** (477 - 524 CE) occupies a unique position as both a terminal figure of the ancient world and a harbinger of **medieval Scholasticism**. His ambitious project to translate and comment on the entire corpus of Aristotle's work, alongside Plato's dialogues, aimed to reconcile the two philosophical giants. Though incomplete, his endeavor preserved much of Greek philosophy through the Dark Ages. "The Consolation of Philosophy," written while Boethius awaited execution, blends Platonic and Stoic philosophies in a dialogue format, offering a meditative exploration on fortune, free will, and the pursuit of the good. Through the character of Lady Philosophy, Boethius converses on the nature of happiness, the impermanence of worldly goods, and the supremacy of philosophical wisdom. This work, immensely popular throughout the Middle Ages and the Renaissance, serves as a crucial conduit for the transmission of ancient philosophy to the Christian intellectual tradition.

Another significant philosophical movement in Late Antiquity was the development of **Neoplatonism**, particularly through the works of Plotinus, Porphyry, and Proclus at the

Alexandrian School. This school sought to systematize Plato's teachings, emphasizing the existence of a singular, ineffable source of all reality, the One. Plotinus' "Enneads" offer a sophisticated metaphysical system where the One emanates the Intellect and the Soul, describing a hierarchical cosmos united by a chain of being stretching from the material to the divine. Neoplatonism deeply influenced Christian, Jewish, and Islamic mysticism, providing a philosophical framework for understanding the nature of God, the soul's ascent towards the divine, and the interconnectedness of all being. The Neoplatonic emphasis on inner spiritual experience and the transcendental nature of the ultimate reality resonated with the mystical dimensions of emerging religious traditions, embedding ancient philosophical concepts into the fabric of Late Antique religious thought.

The contributions of Augustine, Boethius, and Neoplatonism exemplify Late Antiquity's role as a period of intellectual transition and transformation. Their works, bridging the Hellenistic and Christian intellectual worlds, ensured the survival and continuation of classical philosophy in a changing cultural and religious landscape. Through their efforts, the philosophical inquiries of the Greeks were not merely preserved but were also reinterpreted and expanded upon, laying the groundwork for the medieval Scholastic tradition and the Renaissance's humanist revival. Late Antiquity, thus, stands as a testament to the enduring power of philosophical thought to adapt, survive, and flourish across the ages, influencing countless generations in the quest for knowledge and truth.

Late Antiquity also encompasses the rise of Islam, which interacted with the Hellenistic philosophical tradition as Muslim scholars encountered Greek philosophical works. Thinkers like Al-Kindi, Al-Farabi, and Avicenna (Ibn Sina) engaged with Aristotle, Plato, and the Neoplatonists, integrating their ideas into a framework that emphasized reason and revelation's compatibility. This Islamic Golden Age of philosophy ensured the preservation and continuation of Greek thought, which would later be rediscovered in the West during the Renaissance.

The era of Late Antiquity is a testament to the resilience and adaptability of philosophical ideas as they migrate across cultural and religious boundaries. The philosophers of this period laid the groundwork for medieval Scholasticism, the Renaissance revival of classical antiquity, and the enduring dialogue between reason and faith. Their contributions reflect a period of extraordinary intellectual synthesis, where the ancient pursuit of wisdom was enriched by the insights of emerging world religions and new cultural paradigms. In essence, Late Antiquity represents not just a period of transition but a profound transformation in the intellectual landscape of the West. By weaving together the threads of classical philosophy with the rich tapestry of Christian, Jewish, and Islamic thought, the thinkers of Late Antiquity created a legacy that continues to inform our quest for knowledge, meaning, and understanding in the modern world.

## Political Polarization

Augustine's perspective on political polarization would likely be rooted in his views on the City of God versus the City of Man, as outlined in his seminal work, The City of God. Augustine posited that human societies (the City of Man) are inherently flawed and cannot achieve true justice and peace without divine guidance, as people are fundamentally sinful and self-interested after the Fall. From this standpoint, Augustine might see political polarization as a manifestation of humanity's sinful nature and separation from God's will. To address such divisions, Augustine would likely emphasize the need for divine grace and the importance of striving towards the City of God, where peace is based on the love of God rather than the love of self. He would encourage individuals to transcend their immediate political and earthly concerns and focus on living a life of virtue in accordance with Christian teachings, which promote unity, peace, and the common good.

## Environmental Crisis

Both Augustine and Boethius would likely frame the environmental crisis within the context of stewardship and divine order. Augustine's view that nature is a manifestation of God's order and goodness would lead him to advocate for responsible stewardship of the earth. He would argue that humanity has a divine mandate to care for creation, not exploit it, reflecting God's order and benevolence. Boethius might approach the issue through the lens of his discussions on fortune and providence in The Consolation of Philosophy. He could suggest that environmental degradation is partly a result of misaligned human desires and the improper use of fortune. For Boethius, aligning with divine providence involves understanding and embracing the natural order, which includes responsible and ethical treatment of the natural world.

## Rise of Technology

The rise of technology would be scrutinized by Augustine and Boethius through questions about its moral implications and its impact on human souls. Augustine might express concern about technology's potential to lead people away from spiritual matters and towards earthly distractions. He would be wary of technology that enhances human pride and self-sufficiency without acknowledging God's supremacy. Boethius would likely analyze technology from the perspective of its transient benefits versus eternal truths. He might argue that while technology can improve earthly conditions, it should not distract from the pursuit of philosophical wisdom and the contemplation of higher, unchanging realities. Boethius would emphasize the importance of using technology in ways that aid the soul's journey towards understanding and aligning with the divine order.

From the perspective of late antiquity philosophers like Augustine and Boethius, contemporary issues are opportunities to reflect on and realign with divine providence and moral order. They would advocate looking beyond immediate material or political gains towards eternal truths and the ultimate goal of human existence: union with the divine. This approach encourages a holistic view that integrates spiritual, ethical, and practical considerations, aiming to elevate human actions to reflect higher moral and divine principles. Their insights offer profound guidance on navigating modern challenges by focusing on virtues that foster unity, stewardship, and a deeper understanding of our purpose in the cosmos.

# ii. The Islamic Golden Age (~800 CE to ~1300 CE)

The Islamic Golden Age spanned from the 8th to the 14th century, representing a remarkable period of cultural flourishing and intellectual achievement within the Islamic world. This era is characterized by significant advancements in science, technology, medicine, literature, and philosophy. Central to its philosophical contributions was the preservation, translation, and expansion of the Greek philosophical tradition, alongside innovative contributions that would leave a lasting impact on both the Islamic world and the West. The efforts of Muslim scholars during this period not only safeguarded the intellectual heritage of ancient Greece but also set the stage for the Renaissance and the eventual development of modern Western philosophy.

At the heart of the Islamic Golden Age was the Translation Movement, initiated under the Abbasid Caliphate, centered in Baghdad. This movement saw the translation of vast bodies of knowledge, including the works of Plato, Aristotle, Hippocrates, and Galen, from Greek, Syriac, and Persian into Arabic. This monumental task was not merely about preservation but also about making these works accessible for scholarly debate and further inquiry within the Islamic world. The Bayt al-Hikma (House of Wisdom) in Baghdad became a key institution in this intellectual endeavor, attracting scholars of various religious and cultural backgrounds to study, translate, and expand upon the classical heritage. Muslim philosophers engaged deeply with the works of their Greek predecessors, seeking to reconcile and integrate them with Islamic theology.

**Al-Kindi**, often recognized as the first true philosopher of the Islamic world, made significant strides in introducing Greek and Hellenistic thought to the Arab intellectual tradition. Bridging the gap between these diverse cultures, Al-Kindi advocated for the harmony of reason and faith, asserting that true knowledge comes from the integration of philosophical wisdom and divine revelation. His works span a wide array of disciplines, reflecting the holistic nature of his intellectual pursuits. In philosophy, Al-Kindi's treatises on metaphysics and ethics demonstrate a profound engagement with Neoplatonism, adapted within an Islamic framework. His assertion that the intellect is the noblest aspect of a human and his emphasis on the pursuit of knowledge as a way to approach the divine were revolutionary, setting the stage for subsequent Islamic philosophical inquiry.

**Al-Farabi**, known as the "Second Teacher" after Aristotle, contributed extensively to political philosophy, logic, and metaphysics. His visionary work, "The Virtuous City," echoes Plato's "Republic," presenting an ideal society governed by reason and justice under the leadership of a philosopher-king. Al-Farabi's sophisticated commentary on Aristotle's works, especially on logic, played a crucial role in preserving and interpreting the Aristotelian tradition. He posited that an understanding of the natural world and human society is attainable through rational thought, a principle that underpinned his philosophical and scientific endeavors. His influence extended beyond the Islamic world, impacting medieval European philosophy through translations of his works into Latin.

**Ibn Sina**, or Avicenna, stands as a giant in the fields of medicine, metaphysics, and science. His "The Book of Healing" is an encyclopedic work that addresses not only medical sciences but also philosophy, mathematics, and astronomy. Avicenna's "Canon of Medicine" was a seminal text in both the Islamic world and Europe for centuries, revolutionizing medical practice with its systematic approach and empirical basis. In philosophy, Avicenna furthered the understanding of Aristotle's metaphysics, introducing new concepts such as the "necessary being" to argue for the existence of God. His works on the soul, existence, and knowledge contributed to a rich philosophical discourse that bridged the gap between metaphysical speculation and empirical observation.

**Ibn Rushd**, or Averroes, is renowned for his comprehensive commentaries on Aristotle, earning him the title of "The Commentator" in the Latin West. His philosophical writings sought to reconcile Aristotelian philosophy with Islamic theology, advocating for the compatibility of reason and faith. Averroes argued that the pursuit of philosophical knowledge, particularly the study of the natural world and human society, was not only compatible with Islam but was a noble endeavor encouraged by the faith. His defense of philosophy and rational inquiry influenced not only the Islamic tradition but also Christian and Jewish thinkers in medieval Europe, contributing to the development of Scholasticism and, eventually, the Renaissance emphasis on reason and empirical evidence.

The Islamic Golden Age witnessed remarkable achievements in science, mathematics, and medicine, deeply informed by philosophical inquiries into the nature of the universe, the principles of reasoning, and the human condition. The development of algebra by Al-Khwarizmi, the astronomical models of Al-Battani, and the medical insights of Al-Razi (Rhazes) and Avicenna exemplify the era's synthesis of empirical observation with philosophical rigor. The preservation and expansion of Greek philosophy by Islamic scholars during the Golden Age facilitated a cultural and intellectual exchange that transcended geographical and religious boundaries. The transmission of this knowledge to Christian Europe, particularly through the translation of Arabic texts into Latin during the 12th century, played a crucial role in the intellectual awakening that characterized the Renaissance.

## Political Polarization

Philosophers like Al-Farabi, who wrote extensively on the ideal city and the virtuous ruler, would view political polarization as a symptom of leadership that strays from philosophical and ethical ideals. Al-Farabi's concept of the virtuous city involves rulers who possess both practical wisdom and theoretical knowledge, guiding their people toward happiness and virtue. In dealing with modern political polarization, he would likely advocate for education in philosophy and ethics as essential for both leaders and citizens to foster unity and common good. Ibn Rushd, known for his commentaries on Aristotle and his defense of philosophy against theological criticisms, might argue that political polarization results from a lack of rational dialogue and a retreat into dogmatism. He would emphasize the role of philosophical reasoning in public discourse, encouraging a society where diverse viewpoints are examined through the lens of rational critique rather than accepted on authority or tradition alone.

## Environmental Crisis

Ibn Sina's metaphysical and natural philosophy, which includes discussions on the organization of the cosmos and the nature of the soul's relationship to the material world, provides a framework for understanding the environmental crisis. He would likely see environmental degradation as a disorder in the natural world that reflects a deeper metaphysical and ethical imbalance. Ibn Sina might argue for a holistic approach to the environment, one that respects the interconnectedness of all forms of life and the balance crucial for the health of the planet. Al-Kindi, who emphasized the importance of philosophy in understanding and harmonizing the various aspects of human experience, might approach the environmental crisis by highlighting the role of human actions in disrupting the natural balance. He would advocate for a philosophy of balance and harmony, not just within the human soul but between humanity and the natural world.

## Rise of Technology

Al-Kindi, known as the "Philosopher of the Arabs," who wrote on a wide array of subjects including mathematics, astronomy, and medicine, might view modern technology with a keen interest in its potential to enhance human understanding and well-being. However, he would also caution against its misuse that leads to ethical or social harm. Ibn Sina and Al-Farabi might examine the impacts of technology from the standpoint of its effects on the soul and society. They would be interested in how technology can either support or hinder the intellectual and spiritual development of individuals. Their approach would encourage the use of technology to pursue knowledge and virtue but warn against allowing technology to dominate or degrade human capacities.

Philosophers from the Islamic Golden Age would bring a richly nuanced perspective to contemporary issues, grounded in a synthesis of reason, ethical inquiry, and spiritual depth. They would likely advocate for solutions that integrate ethical considerations with practical outcomes, emphasizing the development of knowledge and virtue in both leaders and citizens. Their work reminds us of the importance of maintaining a balance between embracing innovation and preserving moral and spiritual integrity. These philosophers teach us that addressing complex modern issues requires not only technological and political responses but also deep philosophical and ethical reflection.

## iii. The Jewish Philosophical Tradition (~1100 CE to ~1200 CE)

The Jewish Philosophical Tradition, spanning centuries of intellectual inquiry, represents a profound engagement with theological, ethical, and metaphysical questions through the lens of Jewish experience and scripture. This tradition, characterized by a rich dialogue between reason and faith, has contributed significantly to the development of philosophy, particularly during periods of vibrant cross-cultural interaction such as the Islamic Golden Age and the European Middle Ages. Jewish philosophers, engaging with Greek, Islamic, and Christian thought, have navigated the complexities of faith, ethics, and reason, offering unique perspectives that resonate within and beyond Jewish intellectual history.

The Jewish philosophical endeavor, particularly in the medieval period, was significantly shaped by the encounter with Greek philosophy, primarily through Islamic scholarly works. Figures like Saadia Gaon in the 10th century began this engagement, using philosophical methods to defend the Jewish faith and articulate a rational basis for belief and ethical conduct. However, it was in the works of later thinkers such as Moses Maimonides, where this synthesis reached its zenith.

**Moses Maimonides** (1138–1204), also known as Rambam, stands as a colossus in Jewish philosophy and halakhic scholarship. His monumental work, "The Guide for the Perplexed," is a masterful synthesis of Aristotelian philosophy and Jewish theology, aimed at resolving the apparent contradictions between reason and the Torah. Maimonides proposed a method of allegorical interpretation of scripture, suggesting that seemingly anthropomorphic descriptions of God could be understood as metaphorical, aligning with the philosophical conception of God as an immutable, incorporeal being. This approach not only provided a rational foundation for Jewish theology but also opened avenues for dialogue with Islamic and Christian philosophers, contributing to a broader intellectual exchange.

The Jewish philosophical tradition, while deeply engaged with metaphysical questions, has also been characterized by a profound ethical concern. The ethics of the **Halakhah**, Jewish law, grounded in scripture, were subject to philosophical scrutiny and interpretation. Philosophers like Bahya ibn Paquda and Joseph Albo explored the virtues, human purpose, and the nature of divine commandments, integrating ethical discussions with metaphysical insights. The pursuit of ethical living, informed by a philosophical understanding of God's will and the nature of the good, has been a central theme in Jewish philosophy.

In addition to rationalist approaches, Jewish philosophy was also influenced by mystical traditions, particularly **Kabbalah**. The Kabbalistic texts, with their emphasis on the emanative structure of the divine realm and the mystical path to God, offered a different mode of engagement with philosophical questions. The interaction between Kabbalistic mysticism and philosophical rationalism within Jewish thought underscores the tradition's richness and diversity.

The Jewish philosophical tradition has not been insular; it has actively engaged with, influenced, and been influenced by, the broader philosophical currents of the times. In the medieval Islamic world, Jewish thinkers contributed to the intellectual life of the courts and the translation movements. In Christian Europe, Jewish philosophers engaged in dialogue with Christian scholars, participating in the Scholastic debates and the humanist revival of the Renaissance.

The legacy of Jewish philosophy is evident in the enduring questions it poses about faith, reason, ethics, and human nature. In the modern era, thinkers like Martin Buber and Emmanuel Levinas have drawn on this tradition to address contemporary philosophical concerns, including the nature of intersubjectivity, ethics, and the dialogical relationship with the Other.

## Political Polarization

Maimonides placed a strong emphasis on the rational basis of the law (Halakha) and the importance of a harmonious society. He believed that the laws of the Torah were not only divinely inspired but also inherently rational, serving to improve human welfare and promote a just society. In the context of political polarization, Maimonides might advocate for a return to principled, ethical leadership and dialogue grounded in reason and mutual respect. He would likely encourage contemporary leaders and citizens alike to engage in reasoned discourse, emphasizing the values of justice and peace that are central to Jewish thought. Maimonides would likely view the acrimony and division of modern politics as detrimental to the social fabric, suggesting that a focus on shared ethical values and the common good could help bridge divides. His approach would stress the importance of education in both secular and religious contexts to cultivate a more informed and virtuous citizenry capable of meaningful participation in public life.

## Environmental Crisis

Maimonides wrote extensively on the natural world, reflecting the medieval Islamic influence that saw nature as a reflection of divine wisdom. He would likely approach the environmental crisis from the perspective that humanity has a stewardship role over the earth, as suggested by Biblical teachings. This stewardship involves caring for the world in a way that respects its created purpose and ensures its sustainability for future generations. Drawing on Jewish teachings about the sanctity of life and the world as God's creation, Maimonides might advocate for robust environmental ethics that align with both religious obligations and rational public policy. He would argue that just as the law seeks to promote human well-being, so too should it work to prevent environmental degradation that threatens human health and the divine order.

## Rise of Technology

Maimonides lived in an era far removed from modern technology, but his method of integrating Aristotelian philosophy with Jewish theology offers a template for thinking about technological advancements. He would likely be interested in how technology can enhance human understanding and well-being, particularly in fields like medicine and science, which he contributed to in his own work. However, Maimonides would also be cautious about the ethical implications of technology. His work suggests a balance between using technology to improve life and ensuring that it does not lead to moral or spiritual degradation. For instance, he might raise questions about the impacts of social media on community and individual spirituality, or the ethical concerns raised by biotechnology and artificial intelligence. His focus would be on how these technologies can be aligned with the ethical teachings of Judaism and their impact on the soul.

From the perspective of Maimonides and the broader Jewish philosophical tradition, contemporary issues are best addressed through a blend of ethical rigor, rational analysis, and spiritual insight. This approach emphasizes the integration of knowledge across disciplines, the importance of ethical reflection in public policy, and the spiritual dimensions of contemporary challenges. Maimonides teaches us that the solutions to modern problems require not only technological and political responses but also a deep, principled commitment to values that create human dignity, community well-being, and the stewardship of the earth.

# IV. The Medieval Scholastics (~1100 CE to ~1600 CE)

The Medieval Scholastics, flourishing primarily during the High Middle Ages in Europe, represent an integral movement in the history of Western philosophy and theology. Scholasticism, with its distinctive method of inquiry and synthesis, sought to reconcile Christian theology with the philosophical heritage of ancient Greece, particularly the works of Aristotle. This intellectual endeavor was characterized by rigorous dialectical reasoning, aiming to elucidate and systematize complex theological doctrines and philosophical questions within the framework of medieval Christian thought.

Scholasticism's roots can be traced to the monastic schools of the early Middle Ages and later to the cathedral schools and the rise of the first universities in the 12th century. The movement gained momentum with the translation of Aristotle's works into Latin, often from Arabic translations and commentaries by Islamic philosophers like Avicenna (Ibn Sina) and Averroes (Ibn Rushd). These texts introduced medieval European scholars to a comprehensive system of natural philosophy and logic, which they sought to integrate with Christian doctrine.

The Scholastic method was marked by a structured approach to learning and debate, utilizing the "lectio," "quaestio," and "disputatio" techniques. This involved reading authoritative texts, posing questions about them, and engaging in formal debates. Scholastics would cite authorities (auctoritates) such as the Bible, Church Fathers, and classical philosophers to support their arguments, aiming for a synthesis or resolution of differing views.

## Anselm of Canterbury: The Father of Scholasticism (1033 - 1109)

Anselm of Canterbury, often heralded as the father of Scholasticism, pioneered the use of reason in theological inquiry, setting a precedent for the intellectual rigor that would define the Scholastic movement. Born in Aosta, Italy, and later becoming the Archbishop of Canterbury, Anselm's theological and philosophical works sought to understand the truths of Christian faith through reasoned argumentation.

Anselm's most renowned contribution to philosophy is his **ontological argument** for the existence of God, as outlined in his work "Proslogion." The argument posits that the very concept of God as "that than which nothing greater can be thought" necessarily entails God's existence. For Anselm, the ability to conceive of such a being implies that it must exist in reality, as existence in reality is greater than existence in the mind alone. This argument has sparked extensive debate among philosophers, both medieval and modern, with figures like Kant challenging its premises. Yet, its ingenuity and influence on the philosophical proofs for God's existence are undeniable.

Anselm's motto, "fides quaerens intellectum" (faith seeking understanding), encapsulates his approach to theology and philosophy. Unlike some of his predecessors, Anselm did not see a dichotomy between faith and reason but rather believed that faith naturally seeks to understand itself through rational reflection. His works, including "Cur Deus Homo" (Why God Became Man), use logical methods to explore and defend Christian doctrines, such as the necessity of the Incarnation and Atonement. Anselm's efforts to rationalize faith laid the groundwork for subsequent Scholastic thinkers, who continued to explore the compatibility of faith and reason.

## Thomas Aquinas: The Synthesizer of Faith and Reason (1225 - 1274)

Thomas Aquinas, a Dominican friar and theologian, stands as one of the most influential figures in Western philosophy and theology. Aquinas's extensive body of work, most notably the "Summa Theologica," represents a comprehensive effort to reconcile Christian theology with Aristotelian philosophy, asserting the harmony between faith and reason.

In the "Summa Theologica," Aquinas presents his famous Five Ways, rational arguments for the existence of God. These include the argument from motion, causation, possibility and necessity, degrees of being, and the teleological argument. Each argument builds on observable phenomena, employing Aristotelian principles to deduce the existence of an unmoved mover, a first cause, a necessary being, the greatest being, and an intelligent designer. Aquinas's arguments have been pivotal in the natural theology discourse, illustrating his belief in the rational foundations of faith.

Aquinas's contributions to ethics, grounded in his concept of natural law, emphasize the pursuit of the common good and human fulfillment (beatitudo) through virtuous living. For Aquinas, moral law is inscribed in human nature by God and discernible through reason, guiding individuals toward their ultimate end in harmony with the divine will. His integration of Aristotelian virtue ethics with Christian morality offered a robust framework for understanding ethical behavior, influencing moral philosophy up to the present day.

## Duns Scotus: The Subtle Doctor (1266 - 1308)

John Duns Scotus, known as the Subtle Doctor for the intricacy and depth of his thought, was born in Duns, Scotland in 1266 CE. Scotus became a Franciscan friar and theologian, leaving a profound impact on medieval philosophy with his innovative ideas on metaphysics, ethics, and theology.

One of Scotus's significant contributions to philosophy is the concept of the **univocity of being**, which argues that being is predicated in the same way of both God and creatures. This was a departure from the traditional Scholastic view, which maintained a real distinction between the being of God (analogically superior and utterly transcendent) and that of creatures. Scotus's assertion meant that philosophical discussions about being could apply to both God and creation without falling into equivocation, allowing for a more direct discourse on the nature of existence.

Scotus also diverged from Aquinas's intellectualist framework in moral philosophy, emphasizing divine will over intellect. In Scotus's **voluntarism**, the moral law is rooted in the will of God, and moral goodness derives from God's free decision to love and will the good. This perspective underscored the freedom and contingency in God's actions and human moral decisions, offering a nuanced understanding of ethics that highlighted the primacy of love and the will.

Another notable aspect of Scotus's philosophy is his introduction of the concept of **"haecceity"** (thisness), which refers to the principle of individuation that makes an individual distinct from all others. Unlike Aquinas, who attributed individuality to quantitative matter, Scotus proposed that each being has a unique, positive property that confers its individuality. This idea profoundly influenced later discussions on the nature of personal identity and existence.

## William of Ockham: The Invincible Doctor (1285 - 1347/49)

William of Ockham is best known for his advocacy of **nominalism** and the **principle of parsimony**, famously known as **Ockham's Razor**. This principle posits that among competing hypotheses, the one with the fewest assumptions should be selected.

Ockham's nominalism challenged the realist position on universals held by earlier Scholastics, arguing that only individual objects are real, and universals are merely names (flatus vocis) we use to describe a set of observed similarities among things. This radical simplification of metaphysics had profound implications for philosophy and theology, emphasizing a more empirical approach to knowledge and skepticism about the metaphysical speculation of abstract entities.

In addition to his contributions to logic and metaphysics, Ockham also engaged in political philosophy, particularly in the context of the medieval disputes between the papacy and secular rulers. Ockham advocated for the separation of spiritual and temporal powers, arguing that the Church should not wield temporal authority. His views on the limits of papal authority and the importance of poverty for the clergy were influential, reflecting broader debates on the nature of ecclesiastical power and its role in society.

The ripples of Scholasticism extend beyond the Middle Ages, influencing the development of modern philosophy, science, and theology. The Scholastics' commitment to rigorous analysis, structured argumentation, and the integration of faith with reason paved the way for the Renaissance, the Reformation, and the Scientific Revolution. Their endeavors exemplify an enduring aspect of the human intellectual journey: the quest to understand the divine, the natural world, and human existence within a coherent and rational system. Presently, Scholasticism continues to be studied not only for its historical significance but also for its contributions to contemporary philosophical and theological discourse. The Scholastics' exploration of metaphysics, ethics, and the nature of knowledge remains relevant, offering insights into the challenges of synthesizing diverse streams of thought and belief in an increasingly pluralistic world.

The Medieval Scholastics, including Anselm of Canterbury, Thomas Aquinas, Duns Scotus, and William of Ockham, developed their philosophical and theological ideas within the framework of Christianity, seeking to harmonize faith with reason. Their approaches often centered on the principles of natural law, divine providence, and the quest for understanding through rational analysis. This scholastic method can be applied as follows:

## Political Polarization

Thomas Aquinas, perhaps the most influential of the scholastics, might approach political polarization through the lens of natural law and the common good. Aquinas believed that human laws should reflect the natural law, which is grounded in reason and the divine order. In terms of political polarization, he would likely argue for dialogue and policies that are aligned with natural law principles, promoting peace, justice, and the well-being of all members of society. Aquinas would encourage leaders and citizens alike to transcend partisan interests in favor of the universal principles that govern just human conduct. William of Ockham, known for his nominalism and the principle of parsimony (Ockham's Razor), might critique the underlying assumptions that exacerbate political conflicts. He would argue for simplifying complex political issues to their most fundamental elements and addressing them without unnecessary assumptions, focusing on practical solutions that can be universally applied.

## Environmental Crisis

The Medieval Scholastics would likely view the environmental crisis through the concept of stewardship over creation, a common theme in Christian theology. Aquinas, in particular, might argue that humans, endowed with reason, are responsible for maintaining the balance and order of God's creation. This responsibility involves using the Earth's resources wisely and sustainably, ensuring that actions align with both divine will and the natural law principles of preservation and respect for life. Duns Scotus, who emphasized the uniqueness and individuality of every aspect of creation, might highlight the intrinsic value of each creature and ecological system. From his perspective, every part of the environment deserves consideration and protection, as all creation reflects the complexity and generosity of God.

## Rise of Technology

Anselm of Canterbury, known for his ontological argument for the existence of God, would be intrigued by how technology can serve to better understand the divine order and enhance human capabilities. However, he would also caution against using technology in ways that might lead us away from contemplating God and the higher purposes of human existence. Aquinas might evaluate technology based on its ability to contribute to the common good. He would support technologies that improve human welfare, education, and health as consistent with the principles of natural law. However, he would also raise moral questions about technologies that could harm human dignity or disrupt social and ethical norms.

For the Medieval Scholastics, addressing contemporary issues involves a deep engagement with the principles of natural law, the ethical implications of human actions, and the moral responsibilities endowed by divine providence. Their approach combines a robust intellectual inquiry with a profound moral consideration, seeking solutions that are both rational and aligned with Christian ethics. They teach us to look for answers that not only solve practical problems but also elevate the human spirit and promote a deeper understanding of our place in the divine order. Their legacy provides a framework for engaging with modern challenges that require both ethical rigor and rational deliberation, promoting a holistic view of human progress within the cosmic and moral order.

# Chapter 5: Renaissance (~1300 CE to ~1600 CE)

The Renaissance Era, spanning from the 14th to the 17th century, heralded a profound rebirth in art, science, and philosophy, deeply influenced by the rediscovery of ancient texts and the burgeoning spirit of humanism. This period, marked by an exploration of human potential and a renewed interest in the classical past, stands as a testament to the enduring quest for knowledge and the intrinsic value of human creativity and reason. **Leonardo da Vinci**, a polymath who embodied the Renaissance spirit, demonstrated through his work the inseparable link between artistic creativity, scientific inquiry, and philosophical depth. His interdisciplinary exploration underscored the **Renaissance's central thesis (humanism)**: that human beings, equipped with reason and creativity, possess the potential to shape their destiny,

The Renaissance was not merely a historical epoch but a cultural and intellectual movement that sought to harmonize the wisdom of the ancients with the realities of the contemporary world, nurturing a transformative dialogue between past and present. By rediscovering and reinterpreting classical texts, Renaissance thinkers like **Erasmus of Rotterdam** and **Marsilio Ficino** fostered a dialogue across centuries, reaffirming the timeless relevance of philosophical inquiry into ethics and politics.

The humanist movement, epitomized by figures such as **Pico della Mirandola**, emphasized the dignity and potential of the individual, proposing a vision of humanity capable of achieving great intellectual and moral heights. Mirandola's "Oration on the Dignity of Man" encapsulates this spirit, presenting man as a being of boundless capability, poised between the beasts and the angels. This perspective, deeply infused with the values of classical humanism, redefined the moral and political philosophy of the time, advocating for a society that nurtures and celebrates human potential.

The invention of the printing press by Johannes Gutenberg in the mid-15th century played a crucial role in the dissemination of philosophical ideas, making texts more accessible and fostering a broader public engagement with philosophical discourse. This technological innovation facilitated the spread of Renaissance humanism and the critical examination of political and ethical theories, democratizing knowledge in ways that had profound implications for moral and political thought.

The Renaissance also marked a period of increasing challenge to traditional authorities, both religious and secular, as exemplified by the Reformation and the critical scholarship of the period. This questioning of established norms and values was accompanied by a growing emphasis on individualism, reflected in the political philosophies of **Niccolò Machiavelli** and later, **Thomas Hobbes**. Machiavelli's pragmatic approach to statecraft, devoid of the moral idealism of earlier political theories, underscored the complexities of power and governance in a rapidly changing world. The period transformed ancient wisdom, laying the groundwork for the Enlightenment and the development of modern political thought. In terms of moral and political philosophy,, underscores the dynamic relationship between tradition and innovation in the ongoing quest to understand and shape the moral and political contours of our world.

# i. Giovanni Pico della Mirandola (1463–1494)

Mirandola's life and works are a testament to the Renaissance's intellectual ferment and its efforts to reconcile the diverse streams of philosophical thought that flowed from antiquity through the Middle Ages and into the dawn of the modern world. Pico's philosophy, with its ambitious synthesis of various traditions, provides crucial insights into the evolution of moral and political thought, echoing the dialogues initiated by his predecessors and continuing to resonate in contemporary discourse.

Pico's seminal work, the **"Oration on the Dignity of Man,"** is often hailed as the manifesto of Renaissance humanism. In it, Pico presents a vision of human beings as remarkable creatures endowed with the freedom and capacity to shape their own nature through free will and intellectual striving. He posits that humanity, unique in the creation, occupies a special place in the universe, capable of descending to the depths of animalistic urges or ascending to the divine through the pursuit of virtue and wisdom.

In his ambitious "900 Theses," Pico attempted to harmonize the seemingly disparate philosophical, theological, and mystical traditions of the world, including Aristotelianism, Platonism, Stoicism, and the Kabbalah. This endeavor reflected the Renaissance spirit of eclecticism and the belief in a **Prisca theologia** (a perennial philosophy that undergirds all religious and philosophical traditions). Pico's work illustrates the historical imperative to engage in a discourse that transcends temporal and cultural boundaries, seeking universal truths that underpin moral and political philosophy.

Pico's core narrative assumes that humans, through their intellectual and moral efforts, can achieve a state of perfection. This perspective not only celebrates human potential but also imposes a profound ethical responsibility on individuals to strive for self-improvement and virtuous living. Pico's emphasis on human dignity and potential directly contributes to the discourse on moral philosophy, advocating for an understanding of ethics that is grounded in the inherent worth and capabilities of the individual.

While Pico did not directly articulate a detailed political philosophy, his ideas on human dignity, freedom, and potential have significant implications for political thought. The notion that individuals possess the freedom to chart their own course suggests a political order that respects personal autonomy and encourages civic engagement. Moreover, Pico's vision of a harmonious synthesis of diverse philosophical traditions hints at a cosmopolitan ethos, advocating for a political community that values dialogue, tolerance, and the pursuit of common truths across cultural and religious divides.

In sum, Giovanni Pico della Mirandola encapsulates the Renaissance's revolutionary spirit - its reclamation and reinterpretation of past wisdom, its exaltation of human dignity, and its contributions to the canvas of moral and political thought. His work exemplifies the historical imperative to explore, question, and synthesize, offering insights that transcend his time and speak to the universal human condition.

## Political Polarization

Pico della Mirandola would likely approach the issue of political polarization with a focus on the potential for reconciliation and synthesis between opposing views. His philosophical method, which sought to reconcile and find common ground among various schools of thought, suggests that he would advocate for dialogue that bridges ideological divides rather than exacerbates them. Pico believed in the human capacity to ascend to higher levels of understanding and virtue through education and enlightened discourse. In addressing political polarization, Pico would emphasize the transformative power of education in broadening perspectives and fostering a sense of common humanity. He might argue that through learning and dialogue, individuals can come to see beyond their narrow political allegiances to the universal truths that unite all of humanity.

## Environmental Crisis

Regarding the environmental crisis, Pico's views on the dignity and nobility of man suggest that he would see humanity's role as stewards of the Earth as both a privilege and a responsibility. His belief in the ability of humans to shape their destiny and environment through free will and intelligence would lead him to advocate for proactive measures to address environmental degradation. Pico would likely encourage a harmonious relationship with nature that utilizes human creativity and technological innovation to solve environmental problems without compromising the natural world that he saw as a reflection of the divine. His approach would be one of balance, seeking solutions that respect both human ingenuity and the inherent value of the natural environment.

## Rise of Technology

Pico della Mirandola's enthusiasm for human potential and learning suggests that he would view the rise of technology with optimism, seeing it as an extension of human capability and a means to further human progress. However, he would also be mindful of the ethical implications and potential risks associated with technological advancements. Pico would likely advocate for the use of technology to enhance education, communication, and understanding, aligning with his vision of human beings reaching their highest potential. Yet, he would also caution against technology that alienates individuals from one another or from their spiritual and philosophical pursuits. In his view, technology should serve to elevate humanity, helping individuals to achieve their intellectual and spiritual goals, rather than dominating or diminishing human experience.

From the perspective of Giovanni Pico della Mirandola, these challenges are opportunities for demonstrating human ingenuity and the transformative power of reconciliatory philosophy. His optimistic view of human potential drives a belief in our ability to overcome divisions, responsibly steward the natural world, and use technology wisely to enhance the human condition. Pico's legacy teaches us that at the heart of all solutions lies the recognition of human dignity and the limitless capacity for intellectual and moral growth.

## ii. Desiderius Erasmus (1466–1536)

Erasmus of Rotterdam's work, highlighted by an unwavering commitment to scholarly excellence, the purification of Christian belief, and the promotion of peace and understanding, underscores the Renaissance's transformative impact on the discourse surrounding ethics, governance, and human nature. His humanism, characterized by a profound respect for classical languages and an emphasis on moral philosophy as the foundation for personal and societal reform, represents a critical bridge between the classical past and the emerging modern worldview. His advocacy for education and enlightened thought as catalysts for improving individual lives and society at large resonates with the Renaissance's broader intellectual aspirations.

In his satirical masterpiece, **"The Praise of Folly,"** Erasmus employs wit and irony to critique the vices and follies of his time, including the corruption within the Church and the pettiness of scholastic disputations. This work illuminates Erasmus's belief in the power of reason and critical inquiry as tools for moral and social improvement. It challenges readers to reflect on their own beliefs and actions, advocating for a philosophy grounded in humility, tolerance, and a sincere pursuit of truth. His writings on peace, most notably in **"The Complaint of Peace,"** where peace itself laments its treatment at the hands of humanity, highlight his deep-seated opposition to war and conflict. His arguments for peace are not merely moral but also rational, considering the social, economic, and human costs of warfare. This perspective is particularly relevant in discussions of political philosophy, emphasizing the importance of diplomacy, dialogue, and mutual understanding in resolving disputes.

Erasmus's call for the reform of the Church, advocating for a return to the simple, ethical teachings of Christ, highlight his contribution to the discourse on moral philosophy. His emphasis on inner piety over external rituals and dogma advocates for a religion that is lived and experienced directly in the moral choices and actions of the individual. This approach to Christianity, with its focus on ethical conduct and personal responsibility, offers insightful parallels to contemporary discussions on the role of moral values in public life.

Erasmus' emphasis for humanistic education and commitment to ethical reform exemplifies the Renaissance's contribution to the evolution of a discourse that values critical thought, ethical integrity, and the potential for human progress. His vision of a society guided by reason, compassion, and an unwavering commitment to peace offers enduring insights into the challenges and aspirations of the human condition. He embodies the Renaissance's spirit of inquiry and reform, providing a critical link between the moral and political philosophies of antiquity and the evolving thought of the modern world. His intellectual legacy, marked by a profound belief in the power of education, critical thinking, and ethical living, continues to inspire and challenge us to envision a world where knowledge and virtue guide our collective destiny.

## Political Polarization

Erasmus would likely view political polarization with great concern, seeing it as a symptom of a broader decline in moral and intellectual standards. He famously critiqued the abuses of power and the moral failings of both political and religious leaders in his works, advocating for a return to simpler, more genuine Christian values. In addressing modern political divides, Erasmus would emphasize the need for education that not only imparts knowledge but also fosters tolerance, understanding, and a willingness to engage in constructive dialogue. His approach to polarization would involve encouraging leaders and citizens alike to cultivate virtues such as prudence, temperance, and especially charity, which he saw as fundamental to solving disputes and healing divisions. Erasmus would promote the use of eloquent and persuasive rhetoric, not to deceive or overpower opponents, but to reconcile differences and guide people towards a common good.

## Environmental Crisis

While Erasmus did not directly address environmental issues in the way we understand them today, his emphasis on moderation and his criticisms of excess and greed provide a framework for how he might view the environmental crisis. Erasmus would likely condemn the exploitation of the earth's resources due to greed and the pursuit of wealth, which he saw as morally corrupting. He would advocate for a balanced approach to nature, one that respects the bounty of the earth as a gift from God meant to be shared by all humanity. This perspective would align with his Christian humanist views, emphasizing stewardship and responsibility not just for individual gain but for the welfare of the entire human community.

## Rise of Technology

Erasmus's response to the rise of technology would be cautiously optimistic. He was a proponent of the printing press, recognizing its potential to spread knowledge and stimulate intellectual renewal. However, he would also be wary of technology's potential to distract or detract from meaningful human interaction and the deeper pursuit of wisdom. In the context of modern technology, especially digital media, Erasmus would likely focus on the importance of ensuring that these tools enhance, rather than replace, human communication and education. He would advocate for technologies that support learning, disseminate knowledge, and foster understanding across cultures and communities. Yet, he would also caution against becoming overly reliant on technology at the expense of personal reflection and face-to-face interactions, which he valued highly.

Erasmus's approach to contemporary issues from a Christian humanist perspective highlights the importance of education, ethical conduct, and reasoned dialogue in addressing societal challenges. His philosophy suggests that true progress is not just about political solutions or technological advancements but about cultivating a moral and intellectual culture that promotes peace, understanding, and a common commitment to the welfare of all. Through his emphasis on moderate living, responsible leadership, and the transformative power of education, Erasmus provides enduring insights into how we might navigate the complexities of modern life.

## iii. Niccolò Machiavelli (1469–1527)

Niccolò Machiavelli, a figure often cloaked in controversy, stands at the crossroads of Renaissance thought and the emergence of modern political theory. His writings, most notably **"The Prince,"** represent a seminal departure from the moral and political philosophies that preceded him, offering insights that continue to provoke, challenge, and enlighten discussions on governance, power, and human nature. Machiavelli's work, steeped in the complexities of early 16th-century Italian politics, transcends its historical context to engage with timeless questions about the ethics of leadership and the pragmatics of statecraft.

His political philosophy, grounded in a keen observation of human behavior and the dynamics of political power, marks a shift towards a more empirical, if not cynical, view of governance. In "The Prince," he articulates a guide for rulers on acquiring and maintaining political power, advising leaders to be shrewd, pragmatic, and, when necessary, ruthless. This advice, distilled from historical examples and contemporary experiences, showcases Machiavelli's belief in the complexity of political life, where moral ideals often clash with the exigencies of governance.

A central concept in Machiavelli's thought is **virtù**, a term that encompasses qualities such as **strength, wisdom, and strategic acumen**. Unlike the classical conception of virtue as moral excellence, Machiavelli's virtù is instrumental, valued for its efficacy in navigating the treacherous waters of political leadership. This pragmatic reevaluation of virtue challenges traditional ethical frameworks, suggesting that the morality of actions cannot be divorced from their political consequences.

Machiavelli's apparent separation of politics from conventional moral considerations has sparked extensive debate among scholars and ethicists. By arguing that the ends often justify the means, Machiavelli confronts readers with the uncomfortable reality that the pursuit of the common good may necessitate actions that conflict with personal morality. This perspective invites a deeper reflection on the nature of ethical decision-making in the realm of governance, probing the boundaries between personal virtue and political necessity.

Machiavelli's influence extends far beyond the realm of political theory, permeating discussions on leadership, ethics, and human psychology. His unflinching exploration of power, with its insights into the motivations that drive political actors, offers valuable lessons for understanding the complexities of human societies. The term **"Machiavellian,"** often used pejoratively to describe deceitful or manipulative behavior, belies the depth and nuance of Machiavelli's thought, which grapples with the perennial challenges of ethical leadership and the pursuit of justice.

In the contemporary world, where political landscapes are increasingly characterized by volatility and uncertainty, Machiavelli's reflections on power, strategy, and human nature retain their relevance. His work prompts critical questions about the role of ethics in political leadership, the nature of authority, and the responsibilities of the state to its citizens. By challenging readers to consider the pragmatic realities of governance without losing sight of the ideals that inspire and guide political action, Machiavelli contributes to an ongoing dialogue about the foundations of a just and equitable society.

## Political Polarization

Machiavelli would likely view political polarization not primarily as a moral issue but as a practical challenge to state stability and effective governance. He would advise leaders to be astute in managing divisions within the state, using polarization as an opportunity to strengthen their own position and to implement policies that solidify their power and control. Machiavelli might suggest using both manipulation and concession strategically to manage different factions, ensuring that no single group becomes powerful enough to challenge the authority of the state or the leader. In addressing polarization, Machiavelli would emphasize the importance of appearing fair and just while being prepared to act decisively and ruthlessly when necessary. He would advocate for a balance between coercion and persuasion, advising leaders to cultivate public favor while simultaneously ensuring they are feared to a degree that prevents opposition.

## Environmental Crisis

Machiavelli's response to the environmental crisis would likely be pragmatic and geared toward maintaining political advantage and stability. He would view environmental policy through the lens of how it could strengthen the state and its leadership. For example, he might advocate for taking bold environmental actions if they improve the nation's self-sufficiency, reduce dependency on foreign resources, and enhance the ruler's reputation. However, Machiavelli would also be wary of any environmental measures that could weaken a leader's grip on power or provoke unrest among the populace. He would recommend that leaders carefully manage the narrative around environmental issues, ensuring that any policies are framed in a way that they are seen as beneficial for the public and the state, even if the primary motivation is the consolidation of power.

## Rise of Technology

From Machiavelli's viewpoint, the rise of technology would be seen as a powerful tool to be harnessed for enhancing state power and control. He would be particularly interested in technologies that strengthen national security, surveillance, and information dissemination. Machiavelli would advise leaders to control and utilize technology to monitor potential threats, manage public opinion, and disseminate propaganda to maintain stability and prevent insurrection. At the same time, Machiavelli would caution against the uncontrolled spread of technology that could empower rival factions or foreign powers. He would emphasize the need for strategic oversight of technological development and distribution, ensuring that the state remains the primary beneficiary of technological advances.

Machiavelli's approach to contemporary issues offers a perspective that is less concerned with ethical considerations and more focused on practical outcomes and the maintenance of power. His advice would be guided by the principles of realpolitik, advocating for strategies that enhance the strength and stability of the state, even at the expense of moral or ethical norms. This perspective highlights a different dimension of political philosophy, one that prioritizes efficacy and survival over traditional moral values, providing a critical and often stark analysis of power dynamics in modern societies.

# IV. Michel de Montaigne (1533–1592)

Michel de Montaigne stands as **one of the most influential thinkers of the Renaissance**, whose introspective method of inquiry laid the groundwork for the development of modern philosophical thought, particularly the essay as a form of intellectual exploration. Through his seminal work, the "Essays," Montaigne embarked on a profound journey into the self, examining the complexities of human nature, the variability of societal norms, and the foundations of morality and belief. His writings not only reflect the Renaissance's spirit of inquiry and skepticism but also anticipate the concerns and methodologies of contemporary philosophy.

Montaigne's "**Essays**" are a pioneering work in the genre, combining personal reflection, philosophical discourse, and literary experimentation. This form allowed Montaigne to engage with a broad array of topics, ranging from the ethics of friendship and the nature of education to the vagaries of fortune and the experience of death, with a degree of intimacy and immediacy that was revolutionary for its time. His essays are characterized by a conversational tone and a remarkable openness, inviting readers into a dialogue that is both intellectual and deeply human.

A central theme in Montaigne's work is skepticism, a cautious approach to knowledge that questions the certainty of human understanding. Influenced by the ancient Skeptics, Montaigne viewed the pursuit of absolute truth as a futile endeavor, given the limitations of human reason and the diversity of human experiences. This skepticism led him to advocate for intellectual humility and tolerance, principles that resonate strongly in today's pluralistic and often polarized societies.

For Montaigne, the exploration of the self is a fundamental philosophical exercise, one that reveals the complexity and contradiction inherent in human nature. He famously stated, "**I am myself the matter of my book**," underscoring his belief in the importance of self-examination as a path to wisdom. Montaigne's reflections on ethical living are grounded in this introspective practice, emphasizing the role of personal judgment and the experiential basis of moral understanding. His approach to ethics, which values the cultivation of virtues such as moderation, compassion, and honesty, offers a nuanced perspective on the formation of moral character in the face of life's uncertainties.

While Montaigne's contributions to political philosophy are less direct than those of his contemporaries, such as Machiavelli, his work nevertheless provides valuable insights into the governance, justice, and the social contract. His skepticism of dogmatic assertions of authority and his emphasis on the commonalities of human experience serve as a critique of absolutism and a call for political systems that respect individual liberty and dignity. Montaigne's reflections on the relativity of laws and customs challenge readers to consider the foundations of justice and the role of cultural and historical context in shaping political institutions.

His essays continue to be celebrated for their depth, wit, and insight, offering a model for engaging with complex intellectual and ethical issues through the lens of personal experience. Montaigne's embrace of skepticism, his commitment to the exploration of the self, and his advocacy for tolerance and understanding remain as relevant as ever.

## Political Polarization

Montaigne would likely approach the issue of political polarization with a call for moderation and an appreciation for the complexities of human nature. Known for his belief in the fallibility and variability of human reason, Montaigne might caution against rigid ideological commitments and the dangers of dogmatism. In his essays, he often advocated for understanding and tolerance, emphasizing the value of seeing things from multiple perspectives. In the context of modern political divisions, Montaigne would likely recommend a retreat from extreme positions, advocating for a balanced approach that acknowledges the limits of our knowledge and the legitimacy of differing viewpoints. He would stress the importance of civil discourse and the personal cultivation of virtues such as humility and open-mindedness.

## Environmental Crisis

Montaigne's response to the environmental crisis would likely be informed by his deep connection to nature and his broader philosophical skepticism. While not an environmentalist in the modern sense, Montaigne had an acute awareness of the natural world's beauty and complexity, often reflecting on humanity's place within it. He might view the environmental crisis as a symptom of humanity's overreach and arrogance, urging a more respectful and restrained engagement with nature. Drawing from his skeptical philosophy, Montaigne would likely question both overly optimistic technological solutions and apocalyptic predictions, instead advocating for a prudent approach that recognizes the limits of human power and knowledge. He would emphasize the need for personal and collective responsibility in treating the natural world with care and reverence.

## Rise of Technology

Montaigne would approach the rise of technology with characteristic curiosity mixed with caution. He was interested in the broad range of human experiences and inventions, yet he was also wary of claims that place too much faith in human reason and technological progress. Montaigne might be intrigued by the ways technology can enhance understanding and connect people across different cultures and geographies. However, he would also be concerned about technology's potential to distract from genuine self-reflection and meaningful face-to-face relationships. He would likely advocate for a balanced use of technology, one that serves to augment rather than replace the rich complexity of direct human experiences. Montaigne would emphasize the importance of using technology in ways that enhance, rather than diminish, our ability to live thoughtfully and reflectively.

Michel de Montaigne's approach to contemporary issues offers a reflective and deeply humanistic perspective, emphasizing the value of personal judgment, the cultivation of moral virtues, and the acceptance of human limitations. His writings encourage a thoughtful engagement with life's challenges, advocating for moderation, skepticism, and an openness to diverse experiences and viewpoints. Montaigne teaches us that in facing modern complexities, we should strive not only for knowledge and solutions but also for wisdom and understanding, blending a cautious embrace of new possibilities with a profound respect for tradition and the natural world.

# V. Thomas Hobbes (1588 CE - 1679 CE)

Thomas Hobbes, an English philosopher born in the tumultuous era of the English Civil Wars, witnessed firsthand the horrors of a society plunged into chaos and disorder. This historical backdrop profoundly shaped his philosophical inquiries and conclusions, particularly concerning human nature and the role of government. His life's work, rooted in the desire to understand and design the foundations of peace and social order, culminated in his most famous work, "Leviathan," published in 1651. In this seminal text, Hobbes lays out his political philosophy, which has since been foundational in the development of modern political science and moral philosophy.

Hobbes's view of human nature was decidedly pessimistic. He posited that in a state of nature, where no government or law exists, human life would be "solitary, poor, nasty, brutish, and short." According to Hobbes, the natural condition of mankind is a perpetual state of war, where fear and the pursuit of self-preservation drive individuals to live in constant conflict with one another. To escape this dire state, Hobbes argued that individuals collectively agree to surrender their absolute freedoms to a sovereign authority—a Leviathan. This social contract, in Hobbes's view, forms the basis of civil society and government, which are absolute and unchallengeable in their authority but are also the bearers of civil peace and communal order.

In "Leviathan," Hobbes elaborates on the mechanics of human psychology, ethics, and governance, arguing that a strong, undivided government is necessary to restrain humanity's baser instincts. The Leviathan, a metaphorical representation of a supreme ruler or a governing body, holds absolute power, derived from the consent of the governed, who relinquish their rights for the sake of protection and peace. This groundbreaking concept of the social contract challenged the divine right of kings, proposing that legitimate political power must be derived from the consent of the governed, not from divine or hereditary authority.

Hobbes's contributions to moral philosophy are intertwined with his political theories. He believed that moral norms and social contracts are artificial constructs designed to foster cooperative living among naturally self-serving individuals. Morality, in Hobbes's framework, is not a matter of divine command or intrinsic values but a set of agreed-upon rules essential for survival and coexistence. His work initiates crucial debates in moral philosophy regarding the nature of human rights, justice, and the origins of moral obligation. The political realism of Thomas Hobbes, with his emphasis on the needs for authority and security, continues to resonate in contemporary discussions about state power, individual rights, and the balance necessary to maintain social order in modern democracies. His ideas foreshadow later philosophical discussions about government power, civil rights, and the role of the state in ensuring public welfare, making him a pivotal figure in the transition from medieval to modern political theory.

Thomas Hobbes remains a central figure in the canon of moral and political philosophy. His work, particularly the notion of the social contract and the stark portrayal of human nature, challenges us to consider the underpinnings of our political institutions and the values that sustain them. In a world still grappling with the balance between freedom and security, Hobbes's insights are as relevant as ever, reminding us of the complexities inherent in crafting a just and stable society. His philosophical legacy continues to provoke discussion and debate, underscoring the enduring quest to understand and improve the human condition through the structured use of reason and political order.

## Political Polarization

Hobbes would likely view political polarization as a dangerous state that risks devolving into the chaos and violence of the natural state he feared. His solution would advocate for a strong, centralized authority capable of maintaining peace and preventing the dissolution of society into factional conflicts. In Hobbes's view, the sovereign's power must be absolute to be effective; thus, he would likely support measures that strengthen state control and suppress the extreme elements of polarization that threaten societal stability. In the modern context, Hobbes might suggest that political leaders and institutions take decisive actions to enforce laws that curb divisive extremism and maintain public order. He would emphasize the importance of a unified national identity and common goals as essential for the survival and prosperity of the state.

## Environmental Crisis

Hobbes's approach to the environmental crisis would focus on the preservation of peace and societal stability rather than ecological or conservation ethics per se. He would argue that environmental degradation poses a threat to social stability and could potentially lead to conflict over dwindling resources, thus justifying strong governmental intervention to manage environmental issues. Hobbes would likely advocate for a powerful regulatory framework that could enforce sustainable practices and penalize behaviors that endanger the collective security and health of the populace. His emphasis would be on preventing the environmental crisis from undermining the authority of the state and the social contract that binds it together.

## Rise of Technology

Hobbes would approach the rise of technology from a utilitarian perspective, interested in how it can enhance or threaten the power of the sovereign and the stability of the state. He would see positive aspects of technology that strengthen government surveillance and control as beneficial, helping to maintain order and enforce laws effectively. However, Hobbes would also be cautious about technology's potential to empower dissidents and undermine the authority of the state. He would be wary of any technological advances that could lead to a decentralization of power or enable rebellion against the sovereign. Thus, Hobbes might advocate for strict controls and state oversight of technological developments, ensuring they are used to reinforce the social contract and not to disrupt it.

Thomas Hobbes's views provide a framework for addressing contemporary issues through the lens of maintaining social order and the authority of the state. His philosophy underscores the need for strong central governance to manage societal conflicts, environmental challenges, and technological advancements. While his approach prioritizes stability and security, it also raises important ethical questions about the balance between authority and individual freedoms, highlighting the ongoing relevance of Hobbesian thought in modern political and social discourse.

# Chapter 6: Enlightenment (~1600 CE to ~1800 CE)

The Enlightenment, often heralded as the "Age of Reason," emerged as a pivotal epoch that profoundly transformed the intellectual and cultural landscapes of the 17th to 19th centuries. This period, exemplified by a seismic shift towards reason, empirical evidence, and individual rights, stood in stark contrast to the preceding eras, which were dominated by religious dogma, superstition, and the unquestioned authority of monarchies and the Church. The Enlightenment unfolded against the backdrop of significant socio-political changes, including the aftermath of **the Reformation**, the rise of nation-states, and the burgeoning of scientific discoveries that challenged long-held beliefs about the world and humanity's place within it.

The Enlightenment's roots can be traced to the intellectual and scientific advancements of the Renaissance and the political upheavals and religious conflicts that characterized the Reformation. These movements laid the groundwork for a society more open to questioning traditional authorities and exploring new frontiers of thought. The scientific revolution of the 16th century, epitomized by figures like Copernicus, Galileo, and Newton, played a crucial role in this shift, providing a model of inquiry based on observation, experimentation, and the formulation of laws governing the natural world. This empirical approach to knowledge significantly influenced Enlightenment thinkers, who sought to apply similar methods to the study of human society and governance.

As Europe moved into the Enlightenment, the horrors of religious wars and the arbitrary rule of monarchs prompted intellectuals to search for new bases of authority and social order. Thinkers like John Locke in England, Montesquieu in France, and Immanuel Kant in Germany began advocating for governance based on rational principles, the rights of the individual, and the consent of the governed, **challenging the divine right of kings and the centrality of the Church in dictating moral and social norms**.

The Enlightenment was characterized by several core philosophies that collectively represented a departure from the past:

**Empiricism** underscored the importance of sensory experience and observation in the acquisition of knowledge. Figures like **John Locke** and **David Hume** argued that all ideas are derived from experience, challenging the notion of innate ideas and emphasizing the role of the environment and education in shaping the human mind.

**Rationalism**, with philosophers such as **René Descartes** and **Gottfried Wilhelm Leibniz**, posited that reason is the primary source of knowledge and that certain truths can be grasped through intellectual deduction. This approach fostered a belief in the power of human reason to uncover universal truths about nature, society, and morality.

**Liberalism** emerged as a political philosophy advocating for individual freedoms, equality before the law, and the separation of church and state. This was a radical departure from the hierarchical and theocratic societies of medieval Europe, with **Locke's theories of natural rights and government by consent** laying the groundwork for modern democratic thought.

**Secularism** gained prominence as thinkers sought to understand the world and humanity's place in it without recourse to religious explanations. The Enlightenment project aimed at secularizing knowledge, ethics, and politics led to the development of a public sphere where ideas could be debated on rational grounds, independent of religious authority.

The Enlightenment, with its emphasis on reason, empirical evidence, and individual rights, set the stage for profound changes in science, philosophy, and governance. It challenged the old order, proposing new ways of understanding the world and organizing society that would eventually fuel revolutions in America and France and lay the foundations for the modern world. As we explore this era, we learn not only the intellectual achievements of this era but also the challenges and critiques that it faced, both from within and from the movements that followed.

## Enlightenment's Influence on Society and Governance

**The American** (1775–1783) and **the French Revolution** (1789–1799) serve as testament to the Enlightenment's indelible impact on the course of political history. Enlightenment philosophers such as John Locke, Jean-Jacques Rousseau, and Montesquieu provided the intellectual scaffolding for revolutionary thought, advocating for the principles of popular sovereignty, social contract, and the separation of powers. Locke's theories of natural rights and government by consent directly influenced the American Declaration of Independence and the United States Constitution, embedding the ideals of life, liberty, and the pursuit of happiness within the foundation of the nation.

In France, the writings of Rousseau and Voltaire galvanized public sentiment against the absolutism of the Ancien Régime, advocating for a society based on the principles of liberty, equality, and secular governance. The Declaration of the Rights of Man and of the Citizen, a fundamental document of the French Revolution, reflects the Enlightenment's influence in its assertion of universal rights and the legitimacy of governmental authority derived from the will of the people.

The democratic ideals espoused by Enlightenment thinkers emphasized the inherent worth and dignity of the individual, the necessity of rational and just laws, and the importance of governmental accountability to the citizenry. The concept of the rule of law, as opposed to the rule of monarchs or despots, emerged as a guiding principle for the new democratic states, asserting that all members of society, including leaders, are equally subject to publicly disclosed legal codes and processes. The Enlightenment's advocacy for representative democracy, where citizens have a voice in their governance through elected officials, challenged the hereditary monarchies and aristocracies that had dominated Europe. This shift towards democratic governance also underscored the importance of education and public discourse, as an informed citizenry was seen as essential to the health and functionality of a democracy.

This legacy in shaping contemporary society and governance is evident in the global adherence to democratic principles, human rights, and the rule of law. The ideals that fueled the revolutionary movements of the 18th century continue to inspire efforts towards social justice, political reform, and the expansion of democratic governance around the world. However, the realization of Enlightenment ideals remains an ongoing project, fraught with challenges and contradictions. Issues of inequality, disenfranchisement, and the erosion of civil liberties persist, prompting critical reflection on the nature of democracy and the requirements of just governance. The Enlightenment's influence thus serves not only as a historical foundation for modern political systems but also as a source of inspiration and critique in the pursuit of a more equitable, rational, and inclusive world.

# i. John Locke (1632–1704)

John Locke stands as a central figure in the pantheon of Enlightenment thinkers, whose ideas on natural rights, the social contract, and the human mind laid the groundwork for political **liberalism and modern democratic thought**. Locke's philosophical inquiries, articulated in seminal works such as **"Two Treatises of Government"** and **"An Essay Concerning Human Understanding,"** represent a pivotal shift towards individual liberty, equality, and government by consent. His contributions not only challenged the authoritarian structures of his time but also provided a blueprint for the development of liberal democratic societies.

Locke's theory of natural rights emerges as a cornerstone of his political philosophy. He posits that individuals possess inherent rights to life, liberty, and property, which exist prior to and apart from any social or political authority. These rights, according to Locke, are inalienable and must be protected by the government. If a government fails to safeguard these rights or infringes upon them, citizens have the legitimate right to resist and overthrow that government. This revolutionary idea, presented in his "Second Treatise of Government," provided a moral justification for the Glorious Revolution in England and later influenced the framers of the American Declaration of Independence.

Locke's concept of the social contract further elaborates on the relationship between the individual and the state. Contrary to the divine right of kings, Locke argues that **governments are formed by the consent of the governed**, established through a social contract to protect individuals' natural rights. This contract entails a mutual obligation: citizens agree to abide by the laws and decisions of their government, while the government is obligated to respect and protect the citizens' rights. Locke's vision of the social contract as a basis for political legitimacy and authority significantly influenced the development of constitutional democracies, emphasizing the principles of consent, equality, and the rule of law.

In "An Essay Concerning Human Understanding," Locke introduces the concept of the mind as a **"tabula rasa"** or blank slate, arguing against the existence of innate ideas. According to Locke, all knowledge is derived from experience, through the senses and reflection, challenging centuries-old notions about the preexistence of certain truths or principles in the human mind. This empiricist view underscored the importance of education and environment in shaping an individual's beliefs and character, democratizing knowledge and opening the door for the Enlightenment's broader emphasis on reason and empirical evidence as the basis for understanding the world.

Locke's theories of natural rights, the social contract, and the empiricist view of the mind collectively forged a new paradigm in political and philosophical thought. His advocacy for religious tolerance, separation of powers, and government by consent directly contributed to the shaping of liberal political theory and the structure of modern democratic states. Locke's ideas have permeated various declarations of rights and constitutions around the globe, embodying the ideals of freedom, equality, and democracy.

The enduring relevance of Locke's philosophy lies in its appeal to universal principles that transcend time and culture. In contemporary debates on human rights, governance, and the role of the state, Locke's emphasis on individual liberty, consent of the governed, and the importance of protecting natural rights remains a crucial point of reference. His work continues to inspire and challenge, serving as a foundational text for understanding the complexities of modern liberal democracies and the ongoing struggle to balance the needs of the individual with the demands of the community.

In short, John Locke's contributions to Enlightenment thought and his influence on political liberalism and modern democracy are profound and far-reaching. By articulating a vision of rational governance, grounded in the protection of individual rights and the consent of the governed, Locke revolutionized political philosophy and provided the intellectual underpinnings for the democratic values we continue to champion today. His legacy exhibits the transformative power of ideas in shaping human societies.

## ii. Voltaire (1694–1778)

François-Marie Arouet (Voltaire) remains one of the Enlightenment's most formidable and influential figures, known for his sharp wit, profound skepticism, and unwavering commitment to the principles of freedom of speech and religious tolerance. Through a prolific output that spanned plays, poetry, novels, essays, and historical and scientific works, Voltaire became a central figure in the Enlightenment's battle against tyranny, superstition, and the injustices of the Church and state.

Perhaps Voltaire's most enduring contribution to moral and political philosophy is his advocacy for **freedom of speech** and religious tolerance. In his essay **"Treatise on Tolerance,"** Voltaire argues passionately for the respect of religious diversity and the importance of freedom of thought and expression. This work, inspired by the **wrongful execution of Jean Calas** accused of murdering his son to prevent his conversion to Catholicism, exemplifies Voltaire's commitment to combating religious persecution and championing the rights of the individual against the abuses of authority. Voltaire's famous dictum, **"I disapprove of what you say, but I will defend to the death your right to say it,"** though apocryphally attributed, encapsulates his belief in the sanctity of free expression as a cornerstone of a just and enlightened society.

Voltaire's criticisms of the French monarchy and the Catholic Church are well documented in his vast corpus of writings, where he employs satire and irony to expose the corruption, hypocrisy, and ineptitude of the ruling elites. Works like **"Candide"** or **"L'Ingénu"** reveal the absurdities of dogmatism, war, and the social inequalities perpetuated by the collusion between the throne and the altar. Voltaire's relentless critique of the established order made him '**persona non grata**' in France for much of his life, leading to periods of exile where he continued his work from outside the country's borders.

A central theme in Voltaire's oeuvre is the battle against superstition and ignorance, which he saw as the **primary tools of oppression** used by tyrants and clerics alike to maintain their power. His **"Philosophical Dictionary"** is a testament to this fight, offering a scathing analysis of the Church's dogmas and the irrational beliefs that hindered the progress of knowledge and society. Voltaire's advocacy for reason, science, and empirical inquiry contributed significantly to the Enlightenment's broader project of illuminating the darkness of the medieval world with the light of reason and evidence.

As a champion of civil liberties, his influence can be seen in the development of the modern principles of human rights, freedom of expression, and the separation of church and state. His defense of religious tolerance and his critique of fanaticism remain profoundly relevant in today's world, where issues of free speech, religious freedom, and the role of religion in public life continue to provoke debate and conflict. Voltaire represents the quintessential Enlightenment thinker, whose life and work encapsulate the era's ideals of reason, liberty, and the pursuit of happiness. His unwavering defense of free thought and his critique of authoritarianism and superstition provide a critical lens through which to view the challenges and aspirations of the contemporary world. By drawing on Voltaire's insights, we can engage more deeply with the ongoing struggle for freedom, tolerance, and enlightenment in an increasingly complex and divided world.

# iii. Jean-Jacques Rousseau (1712–1778)

Jean-Jacques Rousseau is a complex and pivotal figure in the Enlightenment, whose philosophical works sparked profound debates that reverberated through the French Revolution and into the formation of modern political and educational thought. Rousseau's critique of Enlightenment rationalism and the social structures of his time offered a novel perspective on the nature of freedom, equality, and human society. His contributions, particularly through works like "The Social Contract" and "Émile, or On Education," explore the inherent tensions between individual liberty and societal obligations, laying the groundwork for both contemporary political theory and educational philosophy.

In **"The Social Contract**,**"** Rousseau introduces the concept of the general will as the basis for legitimate political authority. Unlike his contemporaries, who emphasized individual rights and the mechanics of government, Rousseau focused on the moral and spiritual regeneration of society. He argued that true freedom could only be achieved when individuals subordinate their individual wills to the general will, or **the collective desire to achieve the common good**. This radical idea challenged the traditional notions of sovereignty and authority, proposing a form of direct democracy where citizens actively participate in the governance of their community. Rousseau's vision of a society governed by the general will influenced revolutionary thought, particularly in France, providing a philosophical justification for collective action and civic duty.

Rousseau's discourse on the arts and sciences in his first Discourse was a scathing critique of the Enlightenment's uncritical embrace of progress. He argued that the advancements in arts and sciences had led to moral corruption, inequality, and the degradation of human virtues. By valorizing primitive or "natural" man, who lived in harmony with nature and possessed an innate sense of compassion and fairness, Rousseau challenged his contemporaries to reconsider the consequences of civilization and progress. This critique resonated with the growing disillusionment among those who felt marginalized by the rapid changes of the 18th century, sparking a reevaluation of the role of culture, education, and society in fostering human well-being.

In **"Émile, or On Education**,**"** Rousseau revolutionized educational thought by advocating for a child-centered approach that emphasizes the development of the individual's innate goodness and capabilities. Contrasting with the rote learning and strict discipline prevalent in his time, Rousseau proposed that education should be tailored to the natural stages of human development, allowing children to learn through experience and interaction with the world. This groundbreaking work laid the foundations for modern educational theories, emphasizing the importance of fostering curiosity, creativity, and moral development from a young age.

Rousseau's ideas about the social contract and the general will continue to be pivotal in debates about democracy, citizenship, and the rights of the individual versus the needs of the community. Rousseau's emphasis on empathy, compassion, and the inherent goodness of humans offers a counterbalance to more cynical views of human nature, providing a hopeful vision for societal organization and interpersonal relations. Rousseau's contributions highlight the enduring tension between individual freedom and societal obligations, a theme that remains as relevant today as it was in the 18th century. His work challenges us to consider how modern societies can cultivate the virtues of compassion, equality, and active citizenship in the face of ongoing political, social, and technological changes. By engaging with Rousseau's thought, we can explore new pathways toward a more just and humane world, informed by an understanding of our shared humanity and the common good.

# IV. David Hume (1711–1776)

David Hume was a Scottish Enlightenment philosopher, a historian, and an essayist, renowned for his rigorous skepticism and empiricism. Hume's contributions to moral and political philosophy, epistemology, and history profoundly influenced the intellectual landscape of his time and the development of modern thought. His work provides critical insights into human nature, the foundations of morals, and the mechanisms of society and government.

At the core of Hume's philosophy is a profound inquiry into human nature and the mechanisms of human understanding. In his seminal work, **"A Treatise of Human Nature,"** Hume posits that all human knowledge derives from experience, challenging the rationalist traditions that preceded him. He argues that human understanding operates primarily through associations of ideas, which are themselves based on impressions and sensations. This empiricist viewpoint underscores the importance of observation and experience in acquiring knowledge, setting the stage for later philosophical and scientific inquiries that emphasize empirical evidence.

Hume's contributions to moral philosophy are characterized by his emphasis on sentiments as the basis of moral judgments. Contrary to moral rationalists, Hume contends that our ethical evaluations are founded not on reason but on emotion and moral sentiment. In **"An Enquiry Concerning the Principles of Morals,"** he argues that virtues are traits or actions that elicit approval or pleasure in the observer, suggesting that morality is inherently tied to human psychology and the capacity for empathy. This perspective laid the groundwork for utilitarianism and contemporary theories that explore the interplay between emotion and morality.

Hume also introduces the concept of **utility** as a key component of moral virtue, arguing that actions or traits deemed virtuous often contribute to the well-being or happiness of society. This utilitarian aspect of Hume's moral philosophy reflects a pragmatic approach to ethics, where the consequences of actions, in terms of their ability to produce happiness or reduce suffering, are central to moral evaluation.

In his political essays, Hume explores the nature of government, justice, and social institutions, offering a sophisticated analysis of the principles that underlie civil society. He views government as a necessary institution that arises naturally from the needs and interests of individuals living in society. Hume's skepticism about the possibility of a perfect social order led him to advocate for a balanced government that mitigates the flaws of human nature while protecting individual liberty and social stability.

Hume's concept of justice is deeply tied to the conventions and practices that evolve within society to facilitate cooperation and mutual advantage. He argues that **justice and property rights are not innate but are social constructs** that emerge to resolve conflicts and promote the common good. This pragmatic and historically grounded approach to justice and political organization offers valuable insights into the challenges and complexities of designing fair and effective social institutions.

David Hume's legacy is characterized by his commitment to empiricism, skepticism, and a deep appreciation for the complexity of human society. His emphasis on sentiment and utility in moral philosophy challenges us to consider the emotional and psychological dimensions of ethical life, while his analysis of government and justice provides a framework for understanding the evolution and function of social institutions. His insights into human nature, ethics, and politics remain profoundly relevant. His work encourages a critical examination of our assumptions about knowledge, morality, and social organization, inviting a nuanced exploration of the principles that can guide us toward a more just and enlightened world.

## V. Adam Smith (1723–1790)

Adam Smith, known as the father of modern economics, made significant contributions to moral and political philosophy that extend far beyond his seminal work in economic theory. His magnum opus, "The Wealth of Nations," is widely recognized for laying the foundations of economic liberalism, yet it is his less celebrated work, "The Theory of Moral Sentiments," that offers profound insights into human nature, ethics, and social relations. His dual contributions are essential for understanding the close relationship between market forces, moral considerations, and the structure of society.

In **"The Theory of Moral Sentiments**," Smith explores the basis of moral judgments, positing that empathy or "sympathy" is foundational to ethical behavior. He introduces the concept of the **"impartial spectator**," an internalized moral guide that allows individuals to judge their own and others' actions from an objective standpoint. This framework suggests that moral understanding and virtuous conduct emerge from our innate capacity for sympathy and our desire for social harmony and approval. Smith's exploration of moral sentiments emphasizes the complexity of human motivation, challenging the notion that individuals act solely out of self-interest. Instead, he suggests that our social instincts and the desire for mutual respect play crucial roles in shaping moral and ethical norms. This perspective provides a nuanced understanding of the motivations behind human actions, highlighting the interdependence of self-interest and social well-being.

**"The Wealth of Nations"** is perhaps most famous for its articulation of the "invisible hand" metaphor, which describes how individuals' pursuit of self-interest unintentionally promotes the common good through the efficient allocation of resources. Smith argues that when individuals are free to pursue their **own economic interests** within a competitive market, they **contribute to the prosperity and improvement of society as a whole**. This concept has profound implications for political and economic philosophy, advocating for limited government intervention in the economy and emphasizing the benefits of free trade and competition. Smith's analysis of the division of labor, market dynamics, and the role of self-interest in economic exchanges remains foundational for classical and neoclassical economic thought, influencing contemporary debates on globalization, market regulation, and economic policy.

Adam Smith's legacy in moral and political philosophy is characterized by his holistic view of human society, where economic systems, moral considerations, and political institutions are deeply intertwined. His work considers how economic freedoms and market mechanisms intersect with ethical norms and social welfare, providing a rich framework for analyzing contemporary issues. In the context of **modern capitalism**, Smith's insights into the nature of wealth, the importance of sympathy and moral sentiments, and the role of government in regulating economic activity continue to spark debate and reflection. His emphasis on the moral dimensions of economic life challenges us to balance efficiency with equity, competition with compassion, and individual liberty with social responsibility.

# VI. Immanuel Kant (1724–1804)

Immanuel Kant significantly influenced modern philosophy with his rigorous analysis, ethical theory, and critiques of pure reason. Kant's work represents another monumental shift in philosophical thought, introducing a framework for understanding the limits of human knowledge and the conditions of moral action. His critical philosophy, particularly through "Critique of Pure Reason," "Critique of Practical Reason," and "Critique of Judgment," seeks to reconcile the divisions between empiricism and rationalism, science and morality, laying the foundations for a comprehensive system of thought.

In the **"Critique of Pure Reason**,**"** Kant embarks on a profound examination of the faculties of human understanding itself, challenging the assumptions of previous metaphysical inquiries and establishing the boundaries between reason and experience. Kant posits that while our knowledge begins with experience, not all knowledge arises from experience. He introduces the concept of **a priori synthetic judgments**, which are necessary and universal truths that structure our perception and understanding of the world but are not derived from empirical observation. This groundbreaking idea reshaped the epistemological landscape, emphasizing the active role of the human mind in organizing sensory experiences into coherent knowledge.

Kant's moral philosophy, articulated in the "**Critique of Practical Reason**" and "**Groundwork of the Metaphysics of Morals**," centers on the principle of the categorical imperative, which posits that moral actions are those performed out of duty and according to universal laws that one can will to be applied universally. Unlike utilitarian ethics, which judge actions by their consequences, Kantian ethics is **deontological**, focusing on the intention behind actions. Kant argues that moral actions are those that treat individuals as ends in themselves, not as means to an end, thus upholding human dignity and autonomy. This ethical framework has profoundly influenced discussions on human rights, justice, and the ethical responsibilities of individuals and institutions.

In his essay **"Perpetual Peace**,**"** Kant outlines a vision for a peaceful world order grounded in republicanism, the rule of law, and international cooperation. Kant advocates for a federation of free states that could ensure peace through collective security and mutual respect for sovereignty, a precursor to contemporary ideas about international relations and organizations like the United Nations. Kant's political philosophy underscores the importance of democratic governance, individual freedoms, and the ethical conduct of states, themes that resonate with ongoing debates about global justice, human rights, and the conditions for lasting peace.

Kant's famous response, **"Sapere aude"** (Dare to know), to the question of what is Enlightenment? encapsulates the essence of the Enlightenment's call to reason, critical thinking, and intellectual independence. Kant champions the Enlightenment as the process by which humanity emerges from its self-imposed immaturity, advocating for the courage to use one's understanding without guidance from another. This call to intellectual and moral autonomy invites individuals to question authority, challenge tradition, and engage actively in the construction of a rational and just society. His critical philosophy continues to be a cornerstone of modern thought, offering tools to navigate the complexities of knowledge, ethics, and aesthetics. Kant's emphasis on rationality, autonomy, and the intrinsic worth of individuals provides a robust framework for addressing contemporary moral dilemmas and fostering dialogue in an increasingly pluralistic world. Kant's ideas challenge us to confront the limits of our understanding and the imperatives of ethical action, advocating for a reasoned approach to the perennial questions of human existence.

# VII. Jeremy Bentham (1748–1832)

The British philosopher Jeremy Bentham was a jurist, social reformer, and a foundational figure in the development of **modern utilitarianism**. His work radically transformed moral and political philosophy by prioritizing the greatest happiness principle as the basis for ethical decision-making and public policy. Bentham's contributions are of utmost importance to understand the evolution of contemporary thought on justice, rights, and the role of government in ensuring the welfare of its citizens.

At the heart of Bentham's philosophy is the principle of utility, which posits that the rightness or wrongness of actions is determined by their contribution to the greatest happiness or least suffering for the greatest number of people. This principle, articulated in works like **"An Introduction to the Principles of Morals and Legislation**," challenges traditional notions of morality based on divine command or inherent virtues, advocating instead for a pragmatic approach rooted in measurable outcomes and the welfare of society. Bentham's utilitarianism emphasizes the calculation of pleasures and pains, proposing a systematic method for evaluating the moral worth of actions based on their consequences. This approach, often summarized by Bentham's dictum **"it is the greatest happiness of the greatest number that is the measure of right and wrong**," seeks to ground ethical theory and public policy in the empirical assessment of happiness and suffering.

Beyond abstract moral theory, Bentham's work had profound implications for legal and social reforms. He advocated for the **codification of laws and the reform of legal institutions** to make them more efficient, transparent, and equitable. Bentham's critique of common law and his proposals for legal reform aimed at reducing suffering and maximizing social welfare, reflecting his broader commitment to the principle of utility. Bentham was a vocal advocate for human rights, including the abolition of slavery, the decriminalization of homosexuality, and the expansion of democratic rights. His writings on these subjects underscore the application of utilitarian principles to social and political issues, advocating for reforms that enhance the overall happiness and reduce the suffering of individuals and communities.

One of Bentham's most controversial proposals was the **Panopticon**, a design for a prison where inmates are observable by a single guard without being able to tell whether they are being watched. While intended to promote order and discipline through the efficient use of surveillance, the Panopticon has been interpreted as a metaphor for **modern surveillance states**, raising enduring questions about privacy, freedom, and the role of the state in monitoring and controlling the behavior of its citizens.

Hume's development of utilitarianism as a comprehensive ethical framework offers a powerful tool for analyzing moral dilemmas, public policy, and legal principles in terms of their outcomes for human well-being. His ideas continue to influence debates on justice, rights, and the responsibilities of government. The challenges of balancing individual liberties with the common good, addressing global inequalities, and formulating policies on issues from healthcare to climate change are all areas where Bentham's utilitarian approach offers valuable insights. By examining the principle of utility and its application to legal and social reforms, we can explore new pathways toward a society that prioritizes the well-being and happiness of all its members. Bentham's philosophy, with its emphasis on reason, empirical evidence, and the pursuit of happiness, remains a crucial reference point for navigating the ethical and political challenges of the 21st century.

## VIII. Edmund Burke (1729–1797)

The Enlightenment, despite its profound contributions to the development of modern moral and political philosophy, did not go unchallenged. The Counter-Enlightenment, a movement embodied by thinkers like Edmund Burke, arose as a direct critique of Enlightenment rationalism, its perceived disregard for tradition, and its underestimation of social cohesion. The exploration of these critiques provides a nuanced understanding of the Enlightenment's legacy and its limits.

The Counter-Enlightenment represents a reaction against the Enlightenment's emphasis on reason, individualism, and progress. Edmund Burke, a prominent figure in this movement, articulated a compelling critique of the Enlightenment and the French Revolution in his seminal work, **"Reflections on the Revolution in France."** Burke argued that the revolutionaries' reliance on abstract principles of liberty and equality, devoid of historical context and disregard for established institutions, would lead to chaos and tyranny rather than to an ideal society.

Burke championed the value of tradition, prudence, and gradual change, emphasizing the complexity of social institutions and the dangers of radical reform. He posited that societies evolve organically, and that customs and traditions represent accumulated wisdom that guides social cohesion and political stability. Burke's critique of the Enlightenment's rationalist approach highlighted the importance of emotional bonds, cultural heritage, and the unquantifiable aspects of human life that contribute to a society's fabric. Burke's thought has had a lasting impact on **conservative political philosophy** and debates surrounding modernity, progress, and governance. Burke's emphasis on the value of historical continuity, social cohesion, and the cautious reform of institutions resonates with contemporary discussions about the role of tradition in a rapidly changing world.

Counter-Enlightenment thinkers also raised important questions about the limits of human reason and the **potential dangers of utopian thinking**. By challenging the Enlightenment's optimistic view of human perfectibility and the power of reason to remake society, the Counter-Enlightenment contributes to a more balanced understanding of human capabilities and the complexities of social change.

In contemporary discourse, the critiques raised by Counter-Enlightenment thinkers remain relevant as we navigate the challenges of globalization, technological advancement, and cultural homogenization. The tension between tradition and progress, community and individualism, rational planning and organic development, continues to shape political and moral philosophy. The Counter-Enlightenment reminds us of the value of historical context, the wisdom embedded in cultural practices, and the need for humility in the face of complex social dynamics. It challenges the modern world to consider which aspects of Enlightenment thought should be upheld, adapted, or questioned as we strive for a just, stable, and cohesive society.

## Modern Critiques on the Enlightenment

The Enlightenment's enduring influence on society and governance is unquestionable, laying the groundwork for modern principles of democracy, human rights, and scientific progress. However, contemporary critiques of the Enlightenment draw out the complexities and unintended consequences of its legacy, challenging us to reflect on the balance between rationality and other dimensions of human experience. Examining these critiques is essential for a nuanced understanding of our current political and ethical landscape.

One prominent critique centers on the Enlightenment's valorization of reason as the supreme human faculty. Critics argue that this emphasis on rationality can diminish the value of emotions, intuition, and subjective experiences, which are also vital to understanding the human condition and fostering a compassionate society. This critique suggests that the Enlightenment's rationalist agenda may lead to a reductive view of human nature, neglecting the complexity and depth of our emotional and moral lives.

Additionally, the Enlightenment's focus on individual autonomy and rights has also been critiqued for potentially undermining communal bonds and ethical duties to others. While the promotion of individual liberty has been transformative, critics contend that an excessive focus on the individual can erode the sense of community and mutual responsibility essential for social cohesion. This perspective underscores the need for a balanced approach that recognizes both individual rights and our interconnectedness as members of a broader community.

Furthermore, contemporary critiques of the Enlightenment often highlight the dark side of modernity, including colonialism, environmental degradation, and the alienation produced by industrialization. The Enlightenment's narrative of progress and human mastery over nature has been implicated in justifying colonial exploitation and environmental harm. Critics argue that the uncritical pursuit of progress and rational control over the natural world has led to ecological crises and social injustices that threaten global well-being.

These contemporary critiques invite a reevaluation of the Enlightenment's legacy in light of current global challenges. They call for a more holistic approach that integrates rationality with emotional intelligence, respects both individual rights and community values, and promotes a sustainable relationship with the natural world. The Enlightenment's ideals of freedom, equality, and reason remain foundational, but their application must be tempered by an awareness of their limits and potential consequences.

In the context of modern moral and political philosophy, grappling with the critiques of the Enlightenment is crucial for addressing the complexities of the contemporary world. It requires a dialogue that acknowledges the achievements of the Enlightenment while also recognizing its shortcomings and the areas where it must be transcended or reimagined. By engaging with these critiques, "A Discourse on Moral and Political Philosophy in the Contemporary World" contributes to a deeper and more nuanced understanding of how we might navigate the challenges of modernity, striving for a society that honors the full spectrum of human experience and responsibly stewards the planet for future generations.

## Political Polarization, Environmental Crisis, and the Rise of Technology

Political polarization, characterized by the increasing ideological distance and antagonism between political parties, poses significant challenges to democratic societies. Here, we analyze this phenomenon through the lenses of the above philosophers to help us understand their philosophies, and perhaps, the effects of such divisions.

### John Locke

Locke's political philosophy emphasizes tolerance and the role of government in protecting individual rights, including life, liberty, and property. From his perspective, political polarization might be seen as a failure of the social contract, where mutual respect and the pursuit of common interests give way to factionalism and conflict. Locke would likely advocate for a reaffirmation of the principles of liberal democracy that prioritize individual freedoms and the rule of law, mechanisms designed to safeguard against the tyranny of the majority and protect minority opinions within the political spectrum.

Locke's philosophy on property rights and the state of nature provides an intriguing foundation for examining environmental issues. He posited that the Earth and its resources are initially held in common, and individual property rights arise from the labor one invests in these resources. However, Locke also warned against spoilage and emphasized that one should not take more from nature than can be used. From this perspective, Locke would likely argue for sustainable practices that respect the limits of natural resources and prevent environmental degradation that would infringe upon the rights of others to enjoy the same resources.

With regard to the rise of technology, Locke would likely focus on the implications of technology for individual rights and property. He argued that individuals have natural rights to life, liberty, and property, and any technological advancement should enhance these rights. Locke might be particularly interested in issues like digital privacy, considering how personal data and digital property can be protected under his theory of rights. He would advocate for regulations that ensure technology does not infringe on these fundamental rights but instead serves to enhance them.

### Voltaire

Known for his sharp wit and advocacy for civil liberties, Voltaire would critique political polarization through his staunch support for freedom of speech and religious tolerance. He would likely view modern polarization as partly stemming from the intolerance and dogmatism he so vehemently opposed. Voltaire would argue for the importance of education in cultivating reason and critical thinking, reducing the susceptibility of the public to demagoguery and manipulation.

Voltaire's critique of society and authority, often infused with his advocacy for freedom of thought, could be applied to the environmental crisis by challenging dogmatic approaches to economic growth and the exploitation of nature. He would likely emphasize the importance of education and enlightened thinking in addressing environmental issues, promoting science-based policies and criticizing those who ignore scientific consensus on matters like climate change.

Voltaire's advocacy for freedom of thought and expression would lead him to embrace aspects of technology that enhance communication and the spread of information. However, he would also be critical of how technology can be used to manipulate public opinion and infringe on individual freedoms. Voltaire would champion the use of technology to educate and enlighten society, while also warning against its potential to spread misinformation and curb free speech.

## Jean-Jacques Rousseau

Rousseau might interpret political polarization as a symptom of the alienation of individuals from their true nature and from the 'general will,' which represents the collective interests of the community. Rousseau's solution would involve fostering a more direct form of democracy and civic participation to realign individual desires with the general will, thereby reducing factionalism and encouraging consensus-building.

Rousseau's view of civilization's corrupting influence and his idealization of the "noble savage" living in harmony with nature resonate deeply with contemporary environmental ethics. He might argue that modern society's alienation from nature is at the root of the environmental crisis. Rousseau would advocate for a societal transformation that realigns human values with ecological systems and promotes a lifestyle that respects the intrinsic value of the natural world.

Rousseau might view modern technology with skepticism, concerned about its impact on social relationships and its role in further alienating individuals from a more 'natural' state of existence. He would likely critique how technology can contribute to inequality and social fragmentation. Rousseau would emphasize the need for technology to foster genuine communal bonds and support educational practices that bring people closer to nature and each other.

## David Hume

As an empiricist and skeptic, Hume would approach political polarization with caution against the passions that often inflame such divisions. He would emphasize the irrational nature of many political arguments and the role of psychological biases in shaping political beliefs. Hume might suggest fostering a political culture that values skepticism and demands evidence-based arguments to mitigate the influence of irrational passions on political discourse.

Hume's empiricism and his ideas about human passion and reason could be applied to how public perception of environmental issues is shaped. He would likely focus on the role of emotions and psychological biases in shaping our responses to environmental crises. Hume might suggest that fostering a better understanding of the empirical evidence for environmental degradation and promoting rational emotional responses to this evidence are crucial.

Hume would examine the rise of technology from an empirical and psychological perspective, analyzing how it affects human behavior and societal norms. He would be interested in the psychological impacts of technology, particularly how it influences desires, emotions, and actions. Hume might explore the ways technology can be designed to promote rational thinking and mitigate the passions that lead to irrational behavior.

## Adam Smith

While primarily known for his economic theories, Smith's moral philosophy also offers insights into political polarization. He would focus on the lack of sympathy and understanding between opposing political groups. Smith might argue that increasing economic interdependencies and promoting commerce can act as a moderating force, softening extreme views by aligning economic interests across different groups and fostering mutual sympathy among diverse populations.

Smith might view the environmental crisis through the lens of economic systems and their impacts on moral sentiments and vice versa. Known for his invisible hand theory, which suggests that individual self-interest can lead to positive societal outcomes, Smith would be critical of how externalities like pollution are handled. He would advocate for market-based solutions or government interventions that align economic incentives with environmental stewardship.

Smith would analyze the economic implications of technology, particularly how it influences markets and labor. He would see technology as a double-edged sword: on one hand, enhancing productivity and economic growth; on the other, possibly leading to job displacement and increased inequality. Smith would advocate for policies that leverage technological advances to boost economic opportunity and prosperity while also addressing the social costs associated with technological disruptions.

## Immanuel Kant

Kant's philosophy, which centers on the categorical imperative and the autonomy of the individual, would lead him to view political polarization as a failure to respect the inherent dignity of others. Kant would advocate for a public discourse based on principles of rationality, respect, and dignity, promoting dialogue that transcends individual interests and seeks universalizable solutions to political conflicts.

Kant's categorical imperative, which commands that one act only according to that maxim by which you can at the same time will that it should become a universal law, would lead him to condemn actions that harm the environment. Kant would argue that if every individual acted in a way that harmed the environment, the result would be universally detrimental, thus such actions are morally unacceptable. He would advocate for laws and policies that protect the environment as a moral duty to other humans and future generations.

Kant would focus on the moral dimensions of technology, especially how it aligns with his categorical imperative. He would question whether the uses of technology treat individuals as ends rather than means, particularly in contexts like surveillance or data harvesting. Kant would argue for strict ethical guidelines in the development and implementation of technology to ensure that it upholds the dignity of individuals and contributes to the moral progress of society.

## Jeremy Bentham

Bentham's utilitarianism would provide a straightforward metric for evaluating political polarization: does it maximize happiness for the greatest number of people? Clearly, persistent political strife does not meet this criterion. Bentham would likely support political reforms that enhance happiness and well-being, possibly advocating for changes in electoral systems or governance structures to reduce zero-sum political competitions and encourage cooperative, outcome-based politics.

As a utilitarian, Bentham would approach the environmental crisis from the perspective of the greatest happiness principle. He would evaluate environmental policies based on their consequences for human well-being. Bentham would likely support aggressive measures to mitigate environmental impacts that cause widespread suffering and promote policies that ensure the greatest good for the greatest number over the long term.

Bentham would evaluate technology based on its consequences for overall happiness and well-being. He would support technological innovations that provide the greatest good for the greatest number but be wary of technologies that cause harm or suffering, whether directly or indirectly. Bentham would be interested in quantifying the benefits and risks of technology, advocating for utilitarian approaches to regulation and ethical design.

## Edmund Burke

As a conservative thinker, Burke would approach polarization with a focus on the importance of tradition and gradual change. He would caution against radical departures from established political norms and values, arguing that such changes could lead to instability and unpredictability. Burke might suggest that respecting historical institutions and promoting a politics of compromise are key to maintaining social cohesion and political stability.

Burke's emphasis on tradition and his cautious approach to change provide a conservative perspective on environmental issues. He might argue that environmental conservation is consistent with conservative values, emphasizing the preservation of the Earth for future generations as akin to preserving cultural heritage and social institutions. Burke would advocate for a prudent approach that respects the complexities of environmental systems and avoids radical changes that could have unforeseen negative consequences.

Burke would caution against rapid technological changes that disrupt social traditions and norms. He would advocate for a gradual and cautious approach to integrating new technologies into society, ensuring that they do not destabilize established institutions and cultural values. Burke might emphasize the need to balance innovation with the preservation of social cohesion and stability.

The perspectives of these philosophers highlight a spectrum of approaches to understanding and addressing political polarization, the environmental crisis, and impacts of technology on modern society. For political polarization, the perspectives of these philosophers highlight the need for democratic participation, respect for individual rights, and the cultivation of a rational public discourse. They remind us that overcoming deep political divides requires not just political solutions but a recommitment to the core principles of democratic governance and civil discourse. This includes creating an environment where different viewpoints can be expressed and debated within a framework that prioritizes the common good over partisan interests.

In dealing with the environmental crisis, the philosophical insights point to the importance of aligning economic incentives with ecological health and maintaining a deep respect for both human and natural systems. These philosophers advocate for a balanced approach that does not see economic development and environmental sustainability as mutually exclusive but interdependent. Their ideas encourage us to view environmental stewardship not only as a technical or regulatory issue but as a moral and philosophical commitment to future generations and the planet.

When addressing the impacts of technology, one must consider the dual potential of technological advancements to enhance or undermine human welfare. The discourse suggests that managing the rise of technology requires careful consideration of ethical implications, societal impacts, and the preservation of human dignity. Technology should be harnessed to improve human life and societal functions, but not without safeguards that consider potential social disruptions and ethical dilemmas.

Overall, these insights make us realize that tackling modern challenges like political polarization, environmental degradation, and the rapid advancement of technology involves more than just technical solutions; it requires a holistic approach that considers ethical, historical, and practical dimensions. These issues demand a renewed commitment to the foundational values of fairness, dialogue, sustainability, and respect for both human and natural rights. Historical philosophical wisdom helps us better navigate the sophistication of these issues, aiming for solutions that not only solve immediate problems but also contribute to the long-term well-being of humanity and the planet. This balanced approach is essential for ensuring that technological progress, environmental policies, and political reforms enhance rather than compromise the quality of human life and the stability of societal structures.

# Chapter 7: Age of Revolutions (19th to 20th Century)

The Age of Revolutions was a period marked by profound political, economic, and social upheavals which significantly influenced the trajectory of moral and political philosophy. This era, spanning the late 18th through the 19th century, witnessed the industrial revolution's transformative impact on society, the expansion of European empires, and a series of revolutions that reshaped nations and continents. These momentous changes spurred philosophical inquiries that deeply interrogated the nature of freedom, justice, rights, and the human condition, laying the groundwork for modern philosophical thought.

The industrial revolution, originating in Great Britain and spreading across Europe and North America, revolutionized the production of goods and the structure of society. The shift from agrarian economies to industrial manufacturing introduced unprecedented economic growth, but it also brought significant social disruptions. The burgeoning factory system, characterized by harsh working conditions and urban overcrowding, prompted philosophers to grapple with issues of labor rights, economic inequality, and the ethics of capitalism.

Concurrently, the expansion of European empires through colonialism reshaped global dynamics, bringing wealth to European powers while subjecting colonized peoples to exploitation and cultural domination. This era of empire-building raised critical questions about sovereignty, the rights of nations, and the morality of imperialism, challenging philosophers to consider the principles of justice and human dignity on a global scale.

The Age of Revolutions was also defined by pivotal revolutionary movements, most notably the American and French Revolutions, which championed the ideals of liberty, equality, and fraternity. These revolutions not only altered the political landscapes of their respective countries but also inspired a wave of philosophical reflection on governance, democracy, and the social contract. Thinkers such as Edmund Burke, who critiqued the radical impulses of the French Revolution, and Thomas Paine, who defended the principles of democratic revolution, embodied the diverse philosophical reactions to these upheavals.

Amidst these transformations, the quest for universal rights and justice became a central theme of philosophical discourse. The abolitionist movement, the fight for women's suffrage, and the early labor movement emerged as critical arenas for applying and expanding Enlightenment principles. Philosophers like John Stuart Mill, who advocated for women's rights and representative democracy, and Karl Marx, who critiqued the capitalist system and envisioned a classless society, contributed to a rich dialogue on the realization of justice and equity in rapidly changing societies.

As the Age of Revolutions unfolded, its profound transformations, political upheavals, industrial advancements, and the burgeoning of new social orders set the stage for a philosophical introspection that would challenge the very foundations laid during the Enlightenment. This period of intellectual ferment saw the emergence of Existentialism, a philosophical movement that arose in the late 19th and early 20th centuries as a potent response to the disillusionment felt in the wake of modernity's promises. Existentialism, with its emphasis on individual experience, freedom, and the inherent ambiguity of existence, offered a profound critique of the Enlightenment's faith in reason, universal morality, and a fixed human essence. Central figures in this movement, Søren Kierkegaard and Friedrich Nietzsche, spearheaded this reevaluation, laying the groundwork for existential thought.

The existentialist critique of Enlightenment reason, morality, and the essence of human beings inaugurated a philosophical perspective that emphasizes the intrinsic uncertainties of the human condition, the centrality of personal freedom, and the construction of meaning through individual action. This movement profoundly influenced subsequent philosophical thought, literature, and the arts, encouraging a deeper exploration of human subjectivity, existential freedom, and the complexities of living authentically in a contingent world.

The Age of Revolutions, with its dramatic shifts in technology, empire, and governance, catalyzed a period of intense philosophical innovation. The era's challenges; the ethical implications of industrialization, the moral quandaries of colonialism, and the aspirations and risks of revolutionary change, prompted a reevaluation of the foundations of moral and political thought. Philosophers engaged with the complexities of freedom, justice, and human rights, wrestling with the implications of these concepts in a world marked by profound inequality and change.

# i. John Stuart Mill (1806 - 1873)

Jeremy Bentham's Utilitarianism emerged and developed as a powerful ethical framework during the Age of Revolutions, expanding the moral considerations that began during the Enlightenment. Spearheaded by thinkers like John Stuart Mill, Utilitarianism built upon and critically engaged with the ethical legacies of the Enlightenment, introducing a pragmatic approach to morality and governance centered on the maximization of happiness and the minimization of suffering.

John Stuart Mill sought to refine and defend the principles laid out by his predecessor, Jeremy Bentham. Mill's contributions to Utilitarianism are encapsulated in his seminal works, **"Utilitarianism"** and **"On Liberty**," where he articulates a more nuanced version of the doctrine, emphasizing the quality of pleasures over their mere quantity. Mill's assertion that **"it is better to be a human being dissatisfied than a pig satisfied; better to be Socrates dissatisfied than a fool satisfied**," underscores his belief in the intrinsic value of higher intellectual and moral pleasures over baser forms of satisfaction.

Utilitarianism preached 'the principle of greatest happiness,' which posits that actions are right insofar as they tend to promote happiness and wrong as they tend to produce the opposite of happiness. Mill, expanding on Bentham's foundation, argues that this principle should guide not only individual conduct but also the formulation of laws and social policies. The emphasis on happiness and pain as the criteria for moral and political decision-making marked a significant shift towards a more empirically grounded and outcome-oriented approach to ethics and governance.

Utilitarianism, with its focus on the consequences of actions, had a profound impact on social reform movements during the 19th century. Mill, an advocate for **women's rights** and **freedom of expression**, applied Utilitarian principles to argue for social and political reforms that would increase overall happiness and reduce injustice. His defense of individual liberties, particularly **the freedom of thought and speech**, highlighted the role of personal autonomy in achieving a flourishing society.

The influence of Utilitarianism extended beyond specific reforms to shape broader debates on the role of government and the objectives of public policy. Utilitarians argued that the state should play an active role in ensuring the welfare of its citizens, challenging traditional views on government non-intervention. This perspective contributed to the development of welfare policies and legal reforms aimed at alleviating suffering and enhancing the quality of life for all members of society.

By centering happiness and pain as the foundational elements of ethical and political analysis, Utilitarian thinkers like John Stuart Mill profoundly influenced the direction of moral thought and public policy. This emphasis on empirical outcomes and the welfare of the community continues to inform contemporary debates on ethics, justice, and governance. The exploration of Utilitarianism underscores the ongoing relevance of this philosophical tradition in addressing the complex moral challenges of our time, highlighting its enduring legacy in the quest for a more just and compassionate society.

## ii. Karl Marx (1818 - 1883)

Karl Marx emerged as a pivotal figure whose profound critique of industrial capitalism and vision of a classless society introduced a radical shift in the discourse of moral and political philosophy. The development of Marxism during the 19th century provided a trenchant analysis of the economic structures and social relations underpinning capitalist societies, while advocating for a revolutionary overhaul towards socialism and, ultimately, communism. Here we explore Marx's critique of capitalism, his envisioning of a classless society, and the enduring influence of Marxism on political movements and debates concerning justice, equality, and human rights.

Karl Marx, in collaboration with **Friedrich Engels**, articulated a comprehensive critique of capitalism, particularly as it manifested in the newly industrialized economies of Europe. Central to Marx's critique, as outlined in works like **"Das Kapital"** and the **"Communist Manifesto,"** is the concept of class struggle, the engine he believed drove historical development and social change. Marx argued that capitalism, characterized by private ownership of the means of production, inherently produced class divisions between the bourgeoisie (the capitalist class who owns the means of production) and the proletariat (the working class who sells their labor).

Marx critiqued capitalism for its exploitation of the proletariat, where the surplus value created by workers is appropriated by the capitalists as profit, leading to alienation, economic inequality, and periodic crises. He envisioned these contradictions as ultimately leading to capitalism's downfall and the rise of the proletariat in a revolutionary movement to establish a socialist state.

Marx's vision of a classless society, where the means of production are communally owned and each individual contributes and receives according to their ability and needs, represents a radical reimagining of social organization. This vision, articulated in the later stages of Marx's work, envisages the dissolution of class distinctions, the end of exploitation, and the realization of true human freedom and development. Marx believed that **socialism**, as a transitional phase, would pave the way for the emergence of a communist society free from the oppressive structures of capitalism.

The impact of Marxism on political movements and thought has been profound and global. Marx's ideas inspired a wide array of revolutionary movements in the 20th century, from the **Russian Revolution of 1917**, which led to the establishment of the Soviet Union, to anti-colonial movements in Asia, Africa, and Latin America. Marxism provided a framework for analyzing imperialism, economic exploitation, and social injustice, fueling struggles for national liberation, social equality, and workers' rights.

Marxism's contributions to discussions of justice, equality, and human rights are significant, offering a critique of liberal conceptions of rights as abstract and insufficient for addressing **systemic inequalities**. Marxists argue for a conception of justice that addresses the material conditions and social relations that underpin human flourishing. Through its emphasis on economic justice, social solidarity, and the collective organization of society, Marxism challenges us to reconsider the foundations of a just society and the means by which human rights can be universally realized.

Karl Marx's critique of capitalism and his vision of a classless society mark a critical juncture in history, offering a radical perspective on the injustices of modern economic systems and the potential for transformative social change. The legacy of Marxism, with its influence on political movements and its contributions to moral and political philosophy, remains a potent force in contemporary debates on justice, equality, and the realization of human rights. Understanding Marxism is indispensable for grappling with the complexities of economic inequality, social justice, and the pursuit of a more equitable global society.

## iii. Søren Kierkegaard (1813 - 1855)

Søren Kierkegaard, a Danish philosopher, stands out, not just as a harbinger of Existentialism, but as a profound critic of the Enlightenment's overemphasis on rationality and universality. His works offer a deeply personal inquiry into the nature of existence, faith, and the complexities of the human condition, laying the groundwork for existential thought. Kierkegaard's contributions guide our understanding of the shift towards individual experience and the existential dimensions of philosophy.

Kierkegaard's philosophical journey was marked by an intense focus on individuality, subjectivity, and the internal life of the human being. His upbringing, deeply influenced by a melancholic father and the intellectual rigor of his Christian faith, instilled in Kierkegaard a sense of existential dread and a quest for authentic faith. His philosophical project, developed through pseudonymous works and discourses, critiques the prevailing **Hegelianism** of his time, advocating instead for a philosophy that addresses the singular individual in their existential reality.

Kierkegaard's central themes revolve around the concepts of anxiety, despair, and the "leap of faith." In **"Fear and Trembling,"** he introduces the idea of the **"knight of faith,"** an individual who embraces the absurdity of existence and commits to a relationship with the divine beyond the bounds of rational understanding. This "leap of faith" is emblematic of Kierkegaard's critique of the Enlightenment's reliance on reason as the sole pathway to truth. He argues that true faith and understanding require a subjective, passionate commitment that transcends empirical evidence and logical deduction.

Kierkegaard's emphasis on subjectivity as the truth and his exploration of the "self" in works like **"The Sickness Unto Death"** highlight his contributions to discussions of identity, authenticity, and moral responsibility. He posits that individuals are constantly in a state of becoming, tasked with the existential responsibility of defining themselves through their choices and actions. This existential view challenges Enlightenment notions of a fixed human nature, suggesting instead that it is through the struggle with despair, choice, and faith that one attains a sense of self and authenticity.

While Kierkegaard's focus was predominantly on individual existential concerns and Christian ethics, his ideas have profound implications for moral and political philosophy. His critique of mass society and the "crowd," as well as his **skepticism towards** the **unreflective adoption of societal norms**, resonate with contemporary concerns about conformity, freedom, and the ethical implications of political and social structures. Kierkegaard's advocacy for the individual's quest for meaning and moral integrity offers a counterpoint to collective ideologies, emphasizing the importance of personal conviction and ethical living in the face of societal pressures.

# IV. Friedrich Nietzsche (1844 - 1900)

Friedrich Nietzsche presents a radical critique of the foundations of morality, religion, and the philosophical assumptions of his time, including those of the Enlightenment. Nietzsche's profound insights into the **nature of power, morality, and the potential for human transcendence** offer a stark departure from the prevailing norms of moral and political thought. His contributions are examined for their revolutionary impact on our understanding of ethics, governance, and the pursuit of meaning in contemporary society.

Friedrich Nietzsche's philosophical journey was earmarked by a profound skepticism towards traditional values and metaphysical claims. His early exposure to classical philology and his subsequent disillusionment with the academic and religious establishments fueled his philosophical explorations. Nietzsche's body of work, characterized by its **aphoristic style** (compact, condensed and epigrammatic style of writing.) and **incisive critique**, challenges the foundations of Western thought, advocating for a reevaluation of morality, truth, and the significance of human existence.

Nietzsche's critique of morality, most notably articulated in works like "**On the Genealogy of Morals**," contests the Judeo-Christian moral framework and its underlying premises. He argues that conventional moral values are expressions of a "**slave morality**," a defensive mechanism of the weak to assert power over the strong. In contrast, Nietzsche advocates for a "**master morality**," rooted in the affirmation of life, strength, and the "will to power," a fundamental drive to assert and enhance one's force and influence.

Central to Nietzsche's philosophy is the concept of the **Übermensch or Overman**, an individual who transcends the limitations of conventional morality to create new values. The Übermensch embodies Nietzsche's vision for humanity's potential to redefine itself and its world, liberated from the shackles of inherited values and metaphysical constraints. This notion challenges Enlightenment ideals of universal reason and morality, proposing instead a dynamic, individualistic approach to value creation and ethical living.

Nietzsche's concept of eternal recurrence, the idea that one must live one's life as if it would recur in exactly the same form for eternity, serves as a test for the affirmation of existence. It challenges individuals to embrace their lives, with all their suffering and joy, in a manner that they would wish to repeat indefinitely. This radical acceptance and affirmation of life, in all its complexity, represent Nietzsche's antidote to **nihilism,** the sense that life is devoid of meaning.

Nietzsche's philosophical legacy has profoundly influenced modern and contemporary discussions on morality, autonomy, and the nature of political power. His critique of foundational moral principles has inspired a rethinking of ethics that considers the complexities of power, culture, and individual agency. Nietzsche's emphasis on individuality and self-overcoming resonates with contemporary debates on identity, freedom, and the role of the state in facilitating or hindering personal and collective flourishing. By questioning the validity of universal moral values and advocating for the creation of new values rooted in the affirmation of life and power, Nietzsche invites a radical reimagining of the possibilities for human existence and societal organization.

# V. The Abolition of Slavery

The movement to abolish slavery was not merely a political or social crusade but a deeply philosophical endeavor that questioned the very essence of humanity and rights. The abolitionist argument is underpinned by the Enlightenment philosophy of natural rights, which posited that all humans inherently possess rights that are not granted by governments but are intrinsic to human nature. Philosophers like John Locke argued that life, liberty, and property are natural rights, and that any social and political system must be constructed with the preservation of these rights as its most fundamental obligation. This principle directly challenged the institution of slavery, which treated individuals as property rather than persons with rights. The contradiction between the values of emerging liberal democracies and the continued acceptance of slavery necessitated a philosophical reckoning.

Utilitarian philosophers like Jeremy Bentham and later John Stuart Mill argued from a different angle, focusing on the greatest happiness principle. They examined the broader societal impacts of slavery, arguing that the suffering inflicted by slavery far outweighed any economic benefits it provided. From a utilitarian perspective, the abolition of slavery was justified as it would lead to a greater overall good and reduce human suffering, promoting a more equitable distribution of well-being across society. Similarly, Rousseau argued that true freedom could only exist in a society where individuals did not dominate each other, and that all social structures should be based on a contract agreed upon by free individuals. Slavery represents a fundamental violation of this social contract, as it is inherently based on coercion and domination, devoid of any semblance of consent from the enslaved.

The abolitionist movement drew upon these philosophical concepts, articulating a moral vision that transcended legal and economic considerations to address the inherent dignity of every human being. Figures like **William Wilberforce** in Britain, who was influenced by his Christian faith and moral conviction, and **Frederick Douglass** in the United States, whose eloquent articulation of his experiences as a former slave and his philosophical arguments for equality, played pivotal roles in mobilizing public and political support for abolition.

The moral arguments against slavery encompassed a range of philosophical positions, from appeals to Christian ethics and the brotherhood of man to Enlightenment principles of liberty and equality. Abolitionists contended that slavery was a moral abomination that violated the natural rights of individuals and degraded humanity's moral sense. They argued that the institution of slavery was incompatible with the ethical principles of justice and benevolence that should govern human relations.

Central to the abolitionist critique was the concept of human dignity dictated by Kantian ethics. Immanuel Kant's categorical imperative, which instructs that individuals must always be treated as ends in themselves and never merely as means to an end, provided a robust ethical framework that supported abolitionist arguments. Slavery, by its very nature, reduces persons to tools for the realization of others' goals (such as economic profit), blatantly contradicting Kant's principle. This Kantian view voiced a philosophy that emphasized the inherent dignity of every individual, bolstering the moral case against slavery by highlighting its dehumanizing effects.

The abolitionist movement also challenged the legal and institutional frameworks that sustained slavery. Abolitionists advocated for legal reforms and constitutional amendments that would recognize the rights of formerly enslaved individuals and ensure their full participation in the political community. The movement highlighted the contradictions between the democratic ideals of nation-states and the reality of slavery, prompting a reevaluation of the principles of governance and the nature of citizenship. In the United States, the abolition of slavery with the 13th Amendment represented a profound shift in the nation's political philosophy, redefining the scope of liberty and equality under the law. Similarly, in other parts of the world, the gradual abolition of slavery reshaped the political landscape, expanding the concept of who was considered a member of the polity.

The abolition of slavery marks a crucial point of convergence between moral conviction and political action, illustrating the capacity of philosophical ideas to drive social change. It represents a significant achievement in the history of moral and political philosophy, affirming the principles of liberty, equality, and human dignity that continue to inform debates on justice and rights in the contemporary world. The abolitionist movement exemplifies the enduring relevance of philosophical inquiry in addressing the moral challenges of our time and the ongoing struggle for a more just and equitable society.

# VI. The Suffrage Movement

Parallel to the abolition of slavery, the suffrage movement sought to address another grave injustice: the exclusion of women (and, in many contexts, marginalized groups of men) from the political process. Enlightenment thinkers such as **Mary Wollstonecraft** in her seminal work, "**A Vindication of the Rights of Woman**," laid the groundwork by critiquing the rationalizations of gender inequality and advocating for women's education and political participation as rights commensurate with their human dignity. John Stuart Mill, who advocated for women's rights in his essay "**The Subjection of Women**," provided a theoretical framework where he argued that the exclusion of women from voting and political life was a violation of justice and an impediment to societal progress. The suffrage movement, culminating in the early 20th century with the gradual granting of voting rights to women across various nations, was informed by and contributed to debates on democracy, equality, and the role of citizens in governance. This movement exposed the importance of inclusive political institutions and the recognition of women as full members of the political community.

Additionally, using the framework of social contract theory, particularly as expanded by contemporary philosophers like **Carol Pateman** in her critique of traditional contract theory, one can argue that the social contract is only legitimate if all those governed by it have participated in its formulation. Pateman's critique highlights how traditional social contract theory implicitly excluded women by maintaining patriarchal structures under the guise of a supposedly neutral political contract. Including women in the suffrage expands and legitimizes the social contract, ensuring that it truly represents the governed community.

The moral arguments underlying this movement were the principles of equality, justice, and autonomy. Suffragists contended that denying women the right to vote was an affront to their status as moral and rational agents deserving of equal consideration in the polity. This denial was seen as a manifestation of broader systemic injustices that marginalized women and constrained their opportunities for self-determination and participation in public life. The movement mobilized these moral arguments to challenge the status quo and advocate for legal and constitutional reforms that would grant women equal political rights. The philosophical discourse surrounding suffrage emphasized the concept of citizenship as inclusive and egalitarian, advocating for a reconceptualization of the democratic polity to encompass all individuals, regardless of gender.

Politically, Suffragists argued that true democracy could not be achieved while half the population remained disenfranchised. Their advocacy for suffrage was thus intertwined with broader debates about the nature of representation, the role of the citizen in democratic governance, and the ethical foundations of the state. The eventual enfranchisement of women, achieved through relentless campaigning, civil disobedience, and legal battles, marked a significant evolution in political philosophy. It affirmed the principle that democracy must be inclusive and representative of all members of society to be just and legitimate.

One compelling, though less commonly cited, argument for women's suffrage centers on the concept of psychological autonomy and the role of voting in individual development. From this perspective, participating in elections is more than a civic duty; it is a crucial component of personal development and self-realization. Philosophers like John Dewey, who emphasized the interconnection between education and democratic participation, argued that being involved in the democratic process helps individuals grow in self-awareness and maturity. For women, this meant that access to the polls was not just about equality; it was about accessing an essential tool for personal development and empowerment.

Similarly, from an ecological and interdependent perspective, women often bring different priorities and perspectives to political discussions, including a focus on community well-being and sustainability. This view suggests that women are more likely to advocate for policies that consider the long-term health of the environment and the social fabric of communities, which are critical in an increasingly interconnected world facing global challenges like climate change and economic inequality. The inclusion of women in the voting populace, therefore, enhances the diversity of perspectives in policy making, leading to more holistic and sustainable governance.

The suffrage movement is a cornerstone of contemporary discussions on rights, equality, and the democratic process. By articulating and embodying the philosophical principles of equality and justice, the movement contributed immeasurably to the advancement of moral and political philosophy. It challenged and expanded the conceptual boundaries of citizenship and rights, offering profound insights into the nature of democratic participation and the ethical obligations of the polity towards all its members.

They highlight that women's suffrage is not merely a matter of political rights but is integral to societal health, ethical governance, and the holistic development of individuals and communities. By recognizing and integrating these diverse perspectives, we gain a deeper understanding of the profound impacts of the suffrage movement, which continue to resonate in contemporary debates on rights, representation, and the essence of democratic participation.

# VII. The Early Labor Movement

The industrial revolution, while a driver of economic growth, also precipitated severe social inequalities and exploitative labor conditions. The labor movement was underpinned by a diverse array of philosophical influences, ranging from the **utopian socialism of Robert Owen**, who envisioned cooperative communities as a solution to the plight of the working class, to the **dialectical materialism of Karl Marx**, who analyzed the class struggle as the driving force of historical development. These philosophical perspectives provided the intellectual scaffolding for the labor movement, articulating a vision of society in which the rights and dignity of every worker were recognized and respected.

Labor movement's philosophical foundation was the assertion of labor as a fundamental aspect of human existence and the source of all value. This perspective challenged the capitalist system's reduction of **labor** to a mere **commodity**, contending instead that workers, as the creators of wealth, deserved fair compensation, humane working conditions, and a voice in the decisions affecting their lives.

The early labor movement's core tenet was a moral argument that emphasized the inherent dignity of labor and the rights of workers to lead lives of decency and fulfillment. Activists and thinkers within the movement highlighted the dehumanizing conditions of factory work, the exploitation inherent in the wage labor system, and the social alienation produced by industrial capitalism. By drawing attention to these issues, the labor movement positioned itself as a moral crusade against the injustices of the existing economic order. The demand for rights such as a fair wage, reasonable working hours, and safe working conditions was grounded in a broader ethical framework that viewed economic justice as an indispensable component of a just society. This framework advocated for the recognition of workers not merely as economic actors but as individuals with inherent worth and moral claims to the fruits of their labor.

The labor movement also questioned the nature of power and representation within capitalist societies. The establishment of trade unions and the fight for collective bargaining rights were seen as essential means of redressing the power imbalance between workers and employers, providing workers with a mechanism to negotiate their terms of employment and advocate for their interests. Furthermore, the labor movement's calls for social and economic reforms, including the introduction of social security systems, unemployment insurance, and public education, reflected a commitment to a vision of the state that prioritizes the **welfare and dignity of all its citizens**. This vision challenged **laissez-faire capitalism** (a form of free-market capitalism that opposes government intervention in economic affairs) and proposed a more active role for the government in ensuring social justice and economic equality.

Additionally, the labor movement's concerns were not only material but also psychological. The dehumanizing conditions of early industrial labor had profound effects on workers' mental health and overall well-being. Philosophers like Wilhelm Wundt and later psychologists who began to explore the impact of work environments on mental health might argue that improving labor conditions is essential not just for physical health but for psychological health as well. This perspective suggests that fair labor practices are crucial for maintaining a healthy psyche, as they reduce stress, increase job satisfaction, and promote a sense of autonomy and purpose.

Another less discussed aspect is the aesthetic dimension of work, which considers how labor can be a source of beauty and creativity. John Ruskin and William Morris, part of the Arts and Crafts Movement, critiqued the industrial processes that stripped away the craftsmanship and aesthetic enjoyment of production. They argued that the labor movement could advocate not just for better wages and hours but also for the reintroduction of creativity and artistry into the work process. This reintegration would make work not only bearable but also fulfilling and enriching to the human spirit, culminating a sense of pride and craftsmanship.

Furthermore, figures like Henry David Thoreau and later John Muir, who were critical of industrialization's impact on the natural environment, might see the labor movement as an ally in promoting sustainable practices. They could argue that reforms advocated by the labor movement, such as reducing working hours and opposing overproduction, could reduce the ecological footprint of industrial activity. This perspective places the labor movement within the broader context of environmental sustainability, suggesting that fair labor practices are compatible with and supportive of environmental goals..

The early labor movement marks a crucial juncture in the evolution of moral and political philosophy, embodying the struggle for dignity, rights, and justice within the framework of industrial society. It informs contemporary debates on labor rights, economic inequality, and the ethical obligations of societies to ensure the well-being of all members. The movement's historical significance and philosophical contributions offer vital insights into the ongoing endeavor to create a more just and equitable world, where the labor and humanity of every individual are valued and respected.

# Chapter 8: Modern and Postmodern Era (>1900 CE)

Following the Age of Revolutions in the 19th Century, our moral and political philosophical journey transitions into the Modern era of the 20th century and the Contemporary Era of the late 20th and the early 21st century. This period is characterized by rapid technological advancements, global conflicts, existential threats, and significant shifts in the socio-political landscape, leading to new philosophical inquiries and debates. The Modern and Contemporary Era witnesses the emergence of ideologies such as existentialism, postmodernism, feminism, and environmentalism, each offering unique perspectives on morality, politics, and the human condition.

The Modern and Postmodern Reflections era, burgeoning in the wake of profound historical upheavals, marks a critical juncture in the evolution of moral and political philosophy. This period, ensconced within the seismic aftershocks of the Age of Revolutions, is indelibly shaped by the cataclysms of the two World Wars, the ideological binaries of the Cold War, the transformative processes of decolonization, and the complex dynamics of globalization. These monumental events collectively engender a philosophical renaissance, compelling a reevaluation and, at times, a radical overhaul of traditional concepts such as freedom, justice, identity, and ethics.

The 20th century, with its unparalleled scale of conflict, ideological confrontations, and technological advancements, precipitated a crisis in the Enlightenment ideals that had previously anchored philosophical thought. The devastating impact of the World Wars, epitomized by the Holocaust and the atomic bombings, cast a long shadow over notions of human progress and rationality, leading philosophers to question the foundations of Western morality and political structures.

The Cold War era further complicated the philosophical narrative, as the binary opposition between capitalism and communism became a dominant framework for political discourse. This ideological polarization forced a reexamination of concepts like freedom and justice, not only in the context of political governance but also in terms of economic systems and their capacity to fulfill human needs and aspirations. Philosophers grappled with the challenges of advocating for ethical principles in a world increasingly defined by geopolitical tensions and the threat of nuclear annihilation.

The process of decolonization, which saw the dismantling of European empires and the emergence of new nation-states, introduced critical perspectives on the legacy of imperialism and its ethical implications. Philosophers and intellectuals from formerly colonized regions challenged the Eurocentric narratives of history and morality, advocating for a pluralistic understanding of identity, culture, and values. This period witnessed a burgeoning of post-colonial thought, which interrogated the intersections of power, knowledge, and ethics, and sought to articulate visions of justice that transcended the colonial legacy.

The phenomenon of globalization, characterized by the intensified interconnectedness of the world's economies, cultures, and populations, brought forth new philosophical inquiries into the nature of community, responsibility, and rights in a global context. The expanding scope of ethical considerations, now encompassing issues like global inequality, environmental sustainability, and international human rights, reflected a shift towards a more inclusive and interconnected conception of moral and political obligations.

In response to these historical shifts, modern and postmodern philosophers embarked on diverse paths of inquiry, exploring the depths of subjectivity, the constructions of power, and the possibilities for freedom and justice in an increasingly complex world. Postmodern thought, in particular, with its skepticism towards grand narratives and its emphasis on the contingent and constructed nature of knowledge and identity, offered new tools for dissecting the cultural, social, and political legacies of the past and envisioning alternative futures.

The era of Modern and Postmodern Reflections represents a profound engagement with the philosophical questions wrought by a century of conflict, transformation, and interconnection. As we traverse this era, it elucidates the ways in which historical events have irrevocably altered the moral and political thought, prompting philosophers to navigate the tumultuous waters of the modern age with a renewed sense of urgency and a reimagined vision of what it means to live ethically and politically in a rapidly changing world.

# i. Existentialism and Humanism in the Contemporary Era

Existentialism and Humanism emerge as vibrant ideas, embossed with the philosophical exploration of individual experience, freedom, and authenticity. This movement, crystallizing in the mid-20th century amidst the ashes of global conflict and the discontents of modernity, champions a profound reevaluation of human existence, ethical responsibility, and the foundations of societal constructs. Central figures such as **Jean-Paul Sartre** and **Simone de Beauvoir** not only navigate but also illuminate the existential condition, offering profound insights into the human quest for meaning in an ostensibly indifferent universe.

Existentialism posits that existence precedes essence, a revolutionary idea suggesting that individuals first find themselves existing in the world and subsequently forge their essence through actions, choices, and commitments. This philosophy foregrounds the individual's experience of freedom and the inherent angst that accompanies the burden of absolute responsibility for one's fate. Jean-Paul Sartre, in works such as **"Being and Nothingness,"** articulates the existentialist view that humans are condemned to be free, for with the absence of a predetermined human nature comes the onus of shaping one's destiny.

At the heart of existential thought lies the concept of **authenticity**, a state of being wherein the individual lives in accordance with their true self, unencumbered by societal expectations or external impositions. This pursuit of authenticity is intricately linked to the search for meaning, as existentialists argue that **meaning is not found but created** through one's engagement with the world. Simone de Beauvoir, in **"The Ethics of Ambiguity,"** emphasizes the role of individual action in imbuing life with purpose and significance, advocating for a moral framework that acknowledges the ambiguity of the human condition while striving for freedom and solidarity.

Existentialism's emphasis on individual autonomy and self-determination carries profound implications for morality and political thought. Sartre's notion of the **"engaged intellectual"** exemplifies the existentialist commitment to political freedom and social justice, positing that philosophers and writers bear a responsibility to address the pressing issues of their time. Through their existentialist lens, Sartre and Beauvoir critique oppressive systems and advocate for a society that recognizes and nurtures the freedom of every individual. Their works contribute to a broader existentialist dialogue on the ethical responsibilities inherent in freedom, challenging the foundations of traditional moral and political frameworks.

The existentialist dialogue with humanism further enriches the philosophical discourse on ethics, freedom, and the potential for human flourishing. Sartre's **"Existentialism is a Humanism"** defends existentialism against accusations of nihilism, asserting that the philosophy, in recognizing the absence of a divine creator, places the utmost importance on human choice and the ethical imperative to live authentically. This existentialist-humanist synergy highlights a shared conviction in the capacity of individuals to transcend their circumstances and contribute to the creation of a more just and meaningful world.

Today, Existentialism and Humanism continue to offer a potent critique of contemporary societal norms and a compelling framework for understanding individual agency in an increasingly complex world. As societies face new ethical dilemmas posed by technological advancements and global interconnectivity, the existentialist emphasis on personal freedom and responsibility becomes ever more relevant. This philosophy invites a reassessment of how individuals might navigate the existential anxieties of the 21st century, from the alienation wrought by digital landscapes to the existential threats posed by ecological degradation and political instability.

In the digital age, existentialist concerns about authenticity and alienation are acutely pertinent. The mediation of human relationships by technology can obscure genuine interpersonal connections, making Sartre's and Beauvoir's insights into authentic living essential to discussions about online identity and social media's impact on self-perception. The existential challenge today involves distinguishing between one's genuine self and the persona curated for digital consumption. Moreover, the rapid pace of technological change can exacerbate the feeling of **"thrownness,"** a term used by Heidegger (another key figure in existential thought) to describe the individual's sense of disorientation and confusion in being placed into a world without clear meaning or instructions.

Further, as globalization merges diverse cultures and economies, Individuals around the world increasingly confront the existential challenge of finding personal freedom amidst global forces that can seem overwhelming or oppressive. For example, the existential imperative to define oneself can clash with global economic or cultural pressures that impose certain roles or identities. In this context, existentialism provides a philosophical toolset for individuals to assert their freedom against global homogenization and to seek solidarity based on shared human conditions rather than mere cultural or economic alignment. In the existential-humanistic view, our freedom is intertwined with our responsibility to future generations and the planet. This perspective is critical in formulating responses to climate change, advocating not only for individual changes in lifestyle but also for collective action that reflects our shared responsibility for the Earth.

Today, existentialism and humanism continue to inspire a vigorous philosophical dialogue about how individuals might confront the absurdities of existence and the freedoms of self-making in a world that often seems indifferent to human concerns. These philosophies encourage a continual reevaluation of our ethical commitments and our responsibilities towards others, advocating for a life that strives toward authenticity, moral integrity, and solidarity. As we face the challenges of modernity, existentialism and humanism serve as crucial guides, reminding us of the power of human agency in shaping a meaningful and just world.

## Jean-Paul Sartre (1905 - 1980)

Jean-Paul Sartre occupies a central place in the discourse on existentialism, a movement that reshaped modern and postmodern reflections on morality, politics, and the human condition. His work, characterized by a profound exploration of freedom, authenticity, and existential despair, offers pivotal insights into the quest for meaning in an absurd universe and the implications of human agency in crafting ethical and political realities. He is a critical voice in understanding the complexities of contemporary existential and ethical challenges.

Born in Paris in 1905, Sartre's intellectual journey was established by the tumultuous backdrop of the two World Wars, the rise of **Fascism**, and the existential uncertainties of the modern age. Educated at the École Normale Supérieure, Sartre's early encounters with **phenomenology** and his experiences during World War II profoundly influenced his philosophical outlook, leading him to question traditional metaphysical and ethical foundations. His relationship with Simone de Beauvoir, a formidable intellectual in her own right, fostered a lifelong partnership of mutual influence and philosophical exploration.

His core concept is that of **radical freedom**, encapsulated in the assertion that "**existence precedes essence**." For Sartre, human beings emerge into the world without a predetermined nature and are thus free to define themselves through their choices and actions. This freedom, however, is accompanied by an inescapable responsibility, as each decision contributes to the creation of one's essence and the world in which we live. Sartre explores these themes extensively in his magnum opus, "Being and Nothingness," where he delineates the existential condition marked by freedom, angst, and the continuous project of self-definition.

Sartre's exploration of authenticity and the relational dynamics between the self and the "Other" constitutes another cornerstone of his philosophical legacy. In works such as "**No Exit**" and "Being and Nothingness," Sartre examines the ways in which the gaze of the "Other" can objectify the self, leading to experiences of alienation and bad faith. Authentic existence, for Sartre, involves a recognition of one's freedom and a rejection of self-deception, embracing the responsibility to act in accordance with one's genuine desires and values, even in the face of societal pressures.

Sartre's philosophy extends into the realm of political activism and ethical responsibility. His commitment to Marxist principles and his active involvement in political causes, such as the French Resistance and the anti-colonial movement, reflect his belief in the engaged intellectual's role in society. Sartre's later work, "**Critique of Dialectical Reason**," attempts to reconcile existentialism with Marxism, advocating for collective action and solidarity as means to combat alienation and oppression. Moreover, his concept of "**engaged literature**" underscores the potential of art to illuminate social realities and provoke change, highlighting the interconnectedness of ethics, politics, and aesthetics in his thought.

Jean-Paul Sartre's philosophical contributions continue to resonate within contemporary moral and political philosophy. His existentialist framework, with its emphasis on freedom, authenticity, and the ethical dimensions of human action, offers a compelling perspective on the challenges of living meaningfully in an increasingly complex and interconnected world. Sartre's legacy exhibits the enduring relevance of existentialist thought in addressing the existential dilemmas and ethical quandaries of the contemporary era, inviting readers to reflect on the nature of freedom, the responsibilities of intellectual engagement, and the possibilities for authentic existence in the 21st century.

## Simone de Beauvoir (1906 - 1986)

Simone de Beauvoir was a seminal figure in 20th-century existentialist philosophy and feminist thought who profoundly impacted moral and political philosophy with her incisive explorations of freedom, gender, and ethics. Her work, characterized by rigorous analysis and a passionate commitment to equality, challenges traditional notions of femininity and offers groundbreaking perspectives on the social construction of gender and the ethics of liberation. De Beauvoir's contributions are pivotal for understanding the intersections of existentialism, feminism, and contemporary ethical issues.

Her intellectual journey was deeply influenced by her early exposure to existentialist philosophy and her lifelong partnership with Jean-Paul Sartre. Her education at the Sorbonne and subsequent career as a writer, educator, and public intellectual were marked by an unwavering quest to dissect the structures of oppression and advocate for a more equitable world. De Beauvoir's relationship with Sartre, founded on mutual respect and intellectual freedom, facilitated a dynamic exchange of ideas that enriched both their works.

De Beauvoir's seminal work, "**The Second Sex**," published in 1949, represents a foundational text in feminist philosophy, articulating the ways in which women have been historically othered and defined as the "Other" in a male-dominated society. Employing an existentialist framework, de Beauvoir famously asserts, "**One is not born, but rather becomes, a woman**," highlighting the role of societal norms in shaping female identity and experiences. Her analysis extends beyond critique to envisage pathways toward emancipation, advocating for women's freedom to define themselves beyond the constraints of patriarchal definitions.

In "**The Ethics of Ambiguity**," de Beauvoir dives into the existentialist conception of freedom and its ethical implications, arguing that freedom is not only a personal project but also a collective endeavor. She posits that true freedom is achieved only when all individuals are free, emphasizing the interconnectedness of individual actions and the broader social fabric. This work underscores de Beauvoir's belief in the ethical responsibility of individuals to engage in struggles against oppression and injustice, contributing to a vision of an ethically coherent and liberated society.

De Beauvoir's activism and writing were deeply intertwined, as she leveraged her philosophical insights to engage with pressing political issues of her time, including women's rights, anti-colonial struggles, and the fight for sexual freedom. Her advocacy for women's autonomy, reproductive rights, and equality in all spheres of life was instrumental in catalyzing feminist movements in France and beyond. De Beauvoir's life and work exemplify the engaged intellectual, committed to using philosophical inquiry to address the moral and political challenges of the contemporary world.

Her legacy extends far beyond her existentialist roots, influencing diverse fields such as gender studies, ethics, and political theory. Her pioneering analysis of gender as a social construct and her advocacy for existential freedom and ethical responsibility continue to resonate with contemporary debates on identity, equality, and justice. Her contributions underscore the vital role of philosophy in challenging the status quo, envisioning alternative futures, and striving for a world where freedom and dignity are accorded to all individuals, regardless of gender.

Through her life and work, Simone de Beauvoir not only shaped existentialist and feminist thought but also demonstrated the transformative power of philosophy in grappling with the complexities of human existence and striving for a more just and equitable society.

## ii. Postmodernism and Critiques of Meta-Narratives

Postmodernism is a philosophical movement that inaugurated a profound critique of universal truths and grand narratives. This era, typified by its skepticism towards the Enlightenment ideals of reason, progress, and objective knowledge, propels a reevaluation of concepts central to moral and political philosophy. Central to this critique are thinkers like **Michel Foucault** and **Jacques Derrida**, whose works dissect the underpinnings of power, knowledge, and identity, thus challenging the foundational premises of Western thought.

Postmodernism emerged in the latter half of the 20th century as a response to the perceived limitations and totalizing tendencies of modernist thought. It contests the Enlightenment's aspirational narratives of human emancipation through reason and scientific progress, arguing instead for the inherent instability and relativity of knowledge. **Jean-François Lyotard**, in "**The Postmodern Condition**," famously defines postmodernism as "**incredulity towards metanarratives**," positing that the grand narratives of history, science, and culture are insufficient in capturing the multiplicity of human experience and the plurality of truths.

### Michel Foucault (1926 - 1984)

Michel Foucault revolutionized contemporary discourse on **power, knowledge, and subjectivity**. His detailed analyses of societal institutions and discourses have left an indelible mark on moral and political philosophy, challenging conventional narratives and unveiling the complex mechanisms through which power circulates and shapes human experience. Foucault's work allows us to understand the nuances of power dynamics and their implications for ethical and political practices in the contemporary era.

His intellectual trajectory originated from a deep engagement with the complexities of history, psychology, and philosophy. Educated at the École Normale Supérieure in Paris, Foucault was influenced by the existentialist and **phenomenological movements**, though he would eventually chart a distinct philosophical path. His method, characterized by the archaeological and genealogical analysis of discourses and practices, sought to uncover the historical conditions of possibility that underlie our understanding of truth, normalcy, and deviance.

Foucault's core philosophy is the assertion that **power and knowledge are inextricably linked**, each shaping and sustaining the other in the production of truth and social norms. Foucault's concept of power challenges the traditional juridical model, which views power as something that is possessed and exercised explicitly. Instead, he argues that **power is omnipresent, diffused throughout the social body**, and manifested through the norms, discourses, and institutions that govern social life. His studies, notably in works like "**Discipline and Punish**" and "**The History of Sexuality**," demonstrate how disciplinary mechanisms and bio-politics serve to regulate individuals and populations, revealing the capillary nature of power.

Foucault's exploration of subjectivity, particularly in his later work, focuses on the processes through which individuals are constituted as subjects through discursive practices and power relations. He investigates the "**technologies of the self**" that allow individuals to effect transformations in themselves, to attain certain states of happiness, purity, wisdom, or immortality.

Foucault's interest in the care of the self and the aesthetics of existence offers a nuanced understanding of ethics that diverges from traditional normative frameworks, emphasizing the art of living as a practice of freedom.

Foucault's work on power, knowledge, and the subject has profound ethical and political implications, challenging us to reconsider the foundations of our social and political systems. His critique of disciplinary societies and the **normalization of surveillance**, for example, resonates with contemporary concerns about privacy, state control, and the digital panopticon. Foucault's emphasis on the contingency and constructedness of social realities invites a critical examination of the status quo and an ethical commitment to questioning and resistance.

Michel Foucault's legacy extends across disciplines, influencing debates in moral and political philosophy, critical theory, gender studies, and beyond. His conceptual tools, particularly his analyses of power relations and the formation of subjectivities, continue to provide valuable insights into the dynamics of contemporary societies. Foucault's work demonstrates the importance of critical reflection and the perpetual interrogation of the power structures that shape human existence, urging us toward a more reflexive and engaged form of ethical and political practice.

## Jacques Derrida (1930 - 2004)

In postmodern philosophy Jacques Derrida profoundly influences the contours of deconstruction, a method of analysis that interrogates the relationship between text and meaning. His work challenges the traditional anchors of Western thought, such as the **centrality of presence, the stability of meaning**, and the binary oppositions that structure philosophical discourse. Derrida's philosophical inquiries illuminate the complexities of language, ethics, and politics, offering a nuanced critique of foundational concepts and inviting a rethinking of moral and political commitments in the contemporary era.

Born in Algeria, Derrida's philosophical journey was shaped by his engagement with phenomenology and **structuralism**, though he would transcend these influences to establish a distinctive philosophical stance. His approach, known as **deconstruction**, seeks to reveal the inherent instabilities and contradictions within texts, thereby questioning the possibility of absolute meaning or truth. Deconstruction operates by unpacking binary oppositions (such as speech/writing, presence/absence) and demonstrating how these hierarchies depend on undecidable elements that resist full integration into a coherent system.

Derrida's critique of **logocentrism**, the privileging of speech over writing in the Western tradition, underscores his challenge to the metaphysics of presence, the idea that meaning is fully present and accessible in the moment of speech. In works like **"Of Grammatology,"** Derrida argues that writing, traditionally considered secondary to speech, reveals the deferment and difference (différance) that are constitutive of language and meaning. This insight not only disrupts the assumed primacy of speech but also invites a reconsideration of how meaning is constituted and the ways in which philosophical and political concepts are articulated.

Derrida's philosophical project extends beyond linguistic and textual analysis to engage with questions of ethics and politics. His concept of the **"ethics of alterity"** emphasizes the responsibility to the Other as an ethical imperative that precedes ontological determination. This orientation towards the Other challenges conventional notions of identity and community, suggesting that ethical and political relations are founded on an acknowledgment of difference and a receptivity to what lies beyond the self-enclosed subject or polity. In **"The Gift of Death,"** Derrida explores the paradoxes of ethical decision-making and responsibility, highlighting the impossibility of fulfilling all obligations and the necessity of making choices that inevitably exclude some commitments.

Derrida's work has had a profound impact on contemporary moral and political philosophy, critical theory, literary studies, and beyond. His deconstructive method offers a powerful tool for analyzing the discourses and structures that shape our understanding of the world, encouraging a critical stance towards taken-for-granted truths and norms. Derrida's emphasis on undecidability, alterity, and the limits of conceptual frameworks challenges us to approach ethical and political questions with humility, openness, and a constant awareness of the complexities involved. Jacques Derrida's contributions are indispensable for navigating the challenges of the contemporary moment. His work compels us to question the foundations upon which our moral and political commitments rest, to remain attentive to the play of difference and the voices of the marginalized, and to engage with the world in a way that is ethically responsive and politically responsible.

The postmodern critique of meta-narratives and the interrogation of power, knowledge, and identity have significant implications for moral and political philosophy. By dislodging the assumptions of a universal human nature, objective moral values, and the inevitability of progress, postmodernism invites a rethinking of ethical and political frameworks. It emphasizes the contingent, constructed, and contested nature of social realities, advocating for an ethical and political engagement that is attentive to difference, alterity, and the margins of power.

Furthermore, postmodernism's challenge to the grand narratives of emancipation and enlightenment compels a reconsideration of how justice, freedom, and equality are conceptualized and pursued. It suggests that ethical and political action must be rooted in the local, the specific, and the situational, engaging with the complexities and contradictions of contemporary life. Through the work of thinkers like Foucault and Derrida, postmodernism not only interrogates the foundations of Western thought but also opens up new spaces for thinking about ethics, politics, and the possibilities of human coexistence. The exploration of postmodernism underscores the ongoing relevance of questioning, critique, and the relentless pursuit of understanding in an ever-complex world.

## iii. Feminism and Gender Theory

Now we explore the transformative impact feminist thought has had on dismantling entrenched societal norms and reshaping political practices, focusing on the pioneering work of philosophers such as Judith Butler and bell hooks. Their insights not only challenge conventional binaries and power structures but also offer profound critiques and alternatives that resonate within our discourse on moral and political philosophy in the contemporary world.

Feminist philosophy emerges as a critical interrogation of gender's role in structuring society, questioning the foundational assumptions that have historically marginalized women and other gender identities. It scrutinizes the mechanisms through which gender is socially constructed and maintained, advocating for a more equitable distribution of power and the recognition of diverse gender experiences. This philosophical pursuit extends to the analysis of ethical frameworks, urging a reconsideration of moral theories through the lens of gender equity and social justice.

## Judith Butler (1956 - Present)

Judith Butler's work has radically transformed discussions on gender, sexuality, and identity politics. Her contributions offer profound insights into the performative nature of gender and the **fluidity of identity**. This section explores Butler's philosophical journey, her major theoretical contributions, and the implications of her work for moral and political philosophy. Butler's academic journey began with her interest in phenomenology, existentialism, and structuralism. Her engagement with French theorists such as Michel Foucault and Jacques Derrida profoundly influenced her thinking, leading her to interrogate the foundational categories of identity and the social mechanisms that produce and sustain them. Butler's work is characterized by its critical approach to established norms and its exploration of the ways in which power dynamics are embedded in the fabric of social life.

Butler's theory of gender performativity, introduced in her seminal work "**Gender Trouble**" (1990), challenges the notion of gender as a stable and inherent attribute. She argues that **gender is not something one is but something one does**, an ongoing performance shaped by societal norms and expectations. This perspective disrupts the binary conception of gender and opens up possibilities for resistance and subversion by exposing the arbitrary nature of gender categories. By viewing gender as performative, Butler provides a framework for understanding how identities are constructed and maintained through repeated acts and social rituals.

Butler's work extends beyond the analysis of gender to address broader questions of identity, recognition, and social visibility. In "**Bodies That Matter**" (1993) and subsequent works, she examines how regulatory frameworks define the boundaries of intelligibility, determining who is recognized as a subject and who is excluded from the realm of social existence. This interrogation of the politics of recognition highlights the struggles faced by **marginalized communities for visibility and rights**, emphasizing the importance of acknowledging and affirming diverse identities.

Butler's philosophical inquiries have significant ethical and political implications. Her critique of normative frameworks and her advocacy for the fluidity of identity challenge traditional moral assumptions and encourage a reevaluation of ethical practices. Butler emphasizes the ethical responsibility to acknowledge the otherness of the other, advocating for a politics of solidarity and inclusivity. Her involvement in political activism, particularly in the areas of **LGBTQ+ rights** and **anti-war movements**, reflects her commitment to applying philosophical insights to concrete social struggles.

Butler's theories provide critical tools for challenging oppressive structures and imagining new ways of being and relating that transcend normative constraints. Her work serves as a vital reference point for discussions on the complexity of identity, the dynamics of power, and the possibilities for ethical and political transformation in the contemporary era. Judith Butler's philosophical project, with its emphasis on the performative nature of identity and the critique of normative categories, offers invaluable perspectives for navigating the complexities of modern and postmodern life. Her work encourages a continuous questioning of the status quo and a relentless pursuit of a more just and equitable world, where the multiplicities of human existence are recognized and celebrated.

## Bell Hooks (1952 - 2021)

Gloria Jean Watkins (Bell Hooks) was a formidable intellectual force whose wide-ranging contributions spanned **feminist theory, cultural criticism, and educational thought**. Her work, deeply rooted in a **critique of systemic oppression** and an unwavering commitment to **intersectionality**, profoundly impacted discussions on race, gender, and class within moral and political philosophy. Our discourse draws on Hooks' insights to explore the complexities of identity, power, and liberation in contemporary society.

Raised in the segregated South, Hooks' intellectual journey was informed by her experiences of racial and gender oppression. Her early education in **racially segregated schools**, followed by her higher education at Stanford University and the University of California, Santa Cruz, laid the groundwork for her life's work; a dedicated exploration of the intersections of race, capitalism, gender, and their implications for individual and collective freedom.

She is renowned for her critical engagement with mainstream feminist movements, which she argued often neglected the experiences and **voices of women of color, the working class**, and other marginalized groups. In seminal works such as **"Ain't I a Woman: Black Women and Feminism"** and **"Feminist Theory: From Margin to Center,"** Hooks elucidated the necessity of an intersectional approach in feminist theory and practice, one that addresses the multiplicity of oppressions that intersect in the lives of individuals.

One of Bell Hooks' enduring contributions to moral and political philosophy is her articulation of an ethic of love; a transformative force capable of challenging structures of domination and fostering communal solidarity and resilience. In **"All About Love: New Visions,"** she posits love as a pivotal element in the struggle for social justice, advocating for a model of love that is rooted in care, commitment, knowledge, responsibility, and respect. This vision of love as an ethical and political practice offers a counter-narrative to the individualism and alienation prevalent in contemporary society.

Hooks also made significant contributions to the field of education, viewing the classroom as a space of possibility and liberation. Her concept of **"engaged pedagogy,"** outlined in **"Teaching to Transgress: Education as the Practice of Freedom,"** emphasizes education as a practice of freedom that challenges students and teachers alike to critically engage with ideas, question assumptions, and actively participate in the co-creation of knowledge. For hooks, education is integral to the project of **social transformation**, providing a foundation for critical consciousness and empowerment.

She is characterized by her incisive critique of systemic inequalities and her unwavering belief in the potential for **collective liberation**. Her work continues to inspire scholars, activists, and communities, offering a framework for understanding the interconnectedness of social identities and the importance of solidarity in the fight against oppression. Her contributions are invaluable for navigating the challenges of identity, ethics, and politics in a world marked by diversity and division.

In essence, the influence of feminist philosophy on societal norms and political practices is profound and far-reaching. Feminist critique has led to significant legal and social reforms, from the recognition of **women's rights** and **reproductive autonomy** to the challenges against gender-based violence and discrimination. Furthermore, feminist theory has enriched political discourse by introducing concepts such as the **politics of care**, which advocates for a political system that values empathy, interdependence, and the well-being of all community members.

Feminist philosophy's interrogation of traditional ethical and political frameworks encourages a radical reimagining of society, one that prioritizes equality, justice, and the recognition of diverse experiences and identities. The contributions of feminist philosophy illuminate the ongoing struggle for gender justice and the potential for creating more inclusive and equitable forms of communal life. Feminist philosophy provides indispensable insights into the construction of gender, the mechanisms of power, and the possibilities for ethical and political transformation. Their contributions challenge us to critically examine our assumptions, engage with the complexities of identity and difference, and commit to the project of building a more just and inclusive world.

# IV. Environmental Philosophy and Ethics

The maturation of Modern and Postmodern Reflections ushers in a critical examination of humanity's relationship with the natural environment, compelling a philosophical reevaluation of our ethical responsibilities towards the Earth and its myriad forms of life. This era, marked by burgeoning environmental crises such as **climate change, deforestation, and biodiversity loss**, demands a profound shift in ethical perspective; from an anthropocentric worldview to one that recognizes the intrinsic value of all beings and ecosystems. Our discourse integrates these pressing concerns, exploring the evolution of environmental philosophy and the ethical frameworks that advocate for a more sustainable and equitable coexistence with the natural world.

Environmental philosophy represents a pivotal shift in ethical thought, emerging in the latter half of the 20th century as a response to growing concerns over humanity's impact on the natural world. This philosophical movement arose from a critical examination of the prevailing **anthropocentric** ethical frameworks which, historically, have privileged human interests, often relegating the natural environment and non-human life forms to the periphery of moral consideration. The advent of environmental philosophy marks a significant departure from these traditional ethical paradigms, advocating instead for a more holistic approach that recognizes the intrinsic value of all beings and ecosystems.

The genesis of environmental philosophy can be traced back to the post-World War II era, a period characterized by rapid industrialization, technological advancement, and unprecedented environmental change. As societies around the globe experienced the **ecological repercussions of economic growth and development**, a growing contingent of philosophers and thinkers began to interrogate the ethical underpinnings of humanity's relationship with nature. This introspection was fueled by an increasing awareness of the finite nature of Earth's resources and the fragility of its ecosystems, prompting a philosophical inquiry into the moral responsibilities of humans towards the planet.

Two seminal works, Aldo Leopold's **"A Sand County Almanac"** (1949) and Rachel Carson's "Silent Spring" (1962), played a foundational role in catalyzing the environmental movement and inspiring the development of environmental philosophy. Leopold's concept of the **"land ethic,"** advocates for a shift from an anthropocentric to an **ecocentric** worldview, urging humans to see themselves as members of a larger community that includes soils, waters, plants, and animals. This ethical perspective emphasizes the moral significance of the land and its components, advocating for a stewardship model of environmental ethics that respects the interdependence of all life forms. Rachel Carson's **"Silent Spring,"** on the other hand, brought to light the detrimental effects of pesticides on the environment, particularly on bird populations. Carson's meticulous documentation of the ecological and health impacts of chemical pollutants sparked a public outcry and a reevaluation of the regulatory frameworks governing environmental protection. Her work showcased the ethical imperative to safeguard the environment from harm, highlighting the interconnectedness of human health and ecological well-being.

The emergence of environmental philosophy as a distinct field of inquiry has broadened the scope of ethical consideration to include the rights of non-human entities and the moral value of ecological systems. Philosophers and ethicists within this tradition challenge the utilitarian view of nature as merely a resource to be exploited for human benefit. Instead, they advocate for a recognition of the inherent worth of all forms of life and the ecosystems that sustain them. This philosophical perspective has given rise to various ethical frameworks, including deep ecology, ecofeminism, and the ethics of care, each offering unique insights into the complex relationship between humanity and the natural world. These frameworks emphasize the need for a more compassionate and reciprocal interaction with nature, one that acknowledges our dependence on and responsibility towards the Earth and its diverse inhabitants.

Within the narrative of environmental philosophy, a transformative current has emerged, advocating for a profound realignment of humanity's ethical compass towards the natural world. This current, known as **ecocentric ethics**, represents a paradigmatic shift away from anthropocentric viewpoints that valorize human interests above all else. At the heart of this movement is deep ecology, a philosophy that champions the intrinsic value of the natural world, advocating for a holistic and egalitarian relationship between humans and the environment. The inception of deep ecology by Norwegian philosopher **Arne Naess** has catalyzed a reevaluation of the ethical frameworks guiding human interaction with the Earth, positing a radical vision for societal transformation that honors the interconnectedness of all life forms.

Arne Naess introduced the term "**deep ecology**" in 1973, proposing an approach to environmental ethics that transcends the shallow, anthropocentric conservation efforts aimed merely at preserving natural resources for human use. Deep ecology calls for a more profound, philosophical questioning of the underlying values and assumptions that govern human behavior towards the natural world. It **challenges** the prevalent notion of **human supremacy** and the **instrumentalist view** of nature as a commodity, advocating instead for a recognition of the inherent worth of all living beings.

Deep ecology is underpinned by several key principles that collectively form a framework for understanding and acting within the natural world. Central to this framework is the belief in the intrinsic value of all forms of life and the ecological systems that sustain them. This belief necessitates a departure from human-centered ethics towards a more inclusive, **biocentric equality** (the notion that all living beings have equal inherent value, regardless of their utility to humans) that affords moral consideration to the entire biosphere. Deep ecology emphasizes the interdependence and interconnectedness of all life forms, asserting that the well-being of human society is inextricably linked to the health of the planet.

This perspective challenges the anthropocentrism embedded in much of Western thought, which prioritizes human needs and desires at the expense of the natural world. By advocating for biocentric equality, deep ecology calls for a comprehensive reassessment of the ethical considerations that guide human actions, urging a shift towards practices that respect the autonomy and rights of non-human entities.

Deep ecology does not merely critique the prevailing ethical paradigms; it also offers a **vision for societal transformation** that aligns human practices with the principles of ecological harmony and **sustainability**. This vision includes reimagining economic, political, and social structures to support a sustainable coexistence with the natural world. It calls for a radical reduction in human impact on the environment, a reevaluation of consumption patterns, and the adoption of lifestyles and technologies that are in harmony with ecological principles.

The discourse on environmental ethics transcends mere academic speculation, delving into the profound and pressing debates concerning the scope and nature of human responsibilities towards both non-human life and the generations yet to come. This complex web of ethical considerations has given rise to a diverse array of philosophical positions, notably those championed by Peter Singer, Tom Regan, Henry Shue, and Bryan Norton. Each, in their way, has contributed significantly to broadening the ethical landscape, arguing for a more inclusive ethic that extends consideration beyond the immediate human sphere to encompass sentient non-human animals and future human generations.

**Peter Singer** and Tom Regan stand at the forefront of the discourse advocating for the ethical consideration of sentient non-human animals. Singer, through his principle of equal consideration of interests, posits that the capacity for suffering is not confined to humans alone; thus, sentient animals also deserve moral consideration. His argument, articulated in works like "**Animal Liberation**," challenges the speciesist mindset, advocating for an ethical framework that recognizes the suffering of animals and seeks to minimize it. **Tom Regan**, on a parallel trajectory, argues from a rights-based perspective, asserting that animals, as "**subjects-of-a-life**," possess inherent value and are entitled to rights that protect their well-being. Regan's seminal work, "**The Case for Animal Rights**," shifts the conversation from welfare and suffering to the inherent rights of animals, providing a robust ethical foundation for the protection of non-human life from exploitation and harm.

The discourse within environmental ethics also ventures into the realm of **intergenerational justice**, a concept that addresses our ethical obligations to future generations. Philosophers such as Henry Shue and Bryan Norton have been instrumental in highlighting the moral imperatives associated with preserving the planet's health and resources. **Shue**, in his discussions on basic rights and climate justice, emphasizes the duty of the present generation to mitigate environmental degradation to ensure a livable world for future generations. **Bryan Norton**, intertwining environmental ethics with concepts of sustainability, argues for a conservation ethic that values biodiversity and ecological integrity, not only for their utility to humans but as part of our ethical duty to future inhabitants of Earth. Norton's perspective widens the scope of environmental responsibility, merging ecological sustainability with ethical considerations.

The vigorous debates and philosophical positions within environmental ethics serve as a clarion call for reevaluating human responsibilities towards non-human life and future generations. The arguments put forth by Singer, Regan, Shue, and Norton collectively challenge the anthropocentric bias of traditional ethics, advocating for a more inclusive ethical paradigm that recognizes the interconnectedness of all life forms and the continuity of existence across generations.

The escalating threat of climate change has further intensified the ethical discussions within **environmental philosophy**. Philosophers and ethicists grapple with the moral dimensions of climate action, addressing issues of global justice, equitable distribution of responsibilities, and the rights of vulnerable populations disproportionately affected by climate impacts. The ethical discourse on climate change challenges the global community to devise solutions that are not only effective and sustainable but also just and equitable, acknowledging the differential contributions to and impacts of environmental crises.

Environmental philosophy and ethics represent a critical juncture in the broader discourse on moral and political philosophy in the contemporary world. By challenging the anthropocentric paradigms that have historically governed human interaction with the natural environment, this field of inquiry opens up new ethical horizons that prioritize the health of the planet and the well-being of all its inhabitants. In the face of unprecedented environmental challenges, the philosophical reflections and ethical frameworks developed within environmental philosophy offer guiding principles for navigating the complex relationships between humanity, non-human life, and the ecosystems upon which we all depend.

# V. Philosophical Responses to Technological Change

The latter half of the 20th century and the dawn of the 21st have been characterized by an unprecedented acceleration in technological advancements, fundamentally altering the canvas of human existence. The advent of artificial intelligence, biotechnology, and the digital revolution has not only expanded the frontiers of human capability but has also introduced complex ethical and political dilemmas that challenge conventional frameworks of rights, autonomy, and the essence of human nature. In this section we explore the philosophical responses to these technological changes, exploring the multifaceted implications of living in an era defined by rapid technological evolution.

## Ethical Challenges of Artificial Intelligence

The rise of artificial intelligence (AI) has prompted intense philosophical debate over the nature of intelligence, consciousness, and the moral status of AI entities. As machines begin to exhibit capabilities that were once thought uniquely human—from creative expression to decision-making—the question of AI rights emerges as a pressing ethical dilemma. Philosophers like **Nick Bostrom** and **David Chalmers** have engaged with these issues, pondering the potential for artificial consciousness and the ethical obligations humans might owe to sentient machines. Moreover, the deployment of AI in sectors such as healthcare, criminal justice, and employment raises concerns about bias, accountability, and the erosion of human autonomy, urging a reevaluation of ethical principles in the age of machine intelligence.

Nick Bostrom is a distinguished philosopher at the University of Oxford, who has significantly impacted our understanding of AI's potential futures through his seminal work, **"Superintelligence: Paths, Dangers, Strategies**." This book serves as a cornerstone for discussions on the ethical and existential dimensions of advanced AI, offering a meticulous exploration of scenarios where artificial intelligence surpasses human cognitive abilities. Bostrom's analysis is predicated on the assertion that AI's ascension represents one of the most significant existential challenges facing humanity. He meticulously outlines the various pathways through which AI could achieve superintelligence and the potential risks associated with each. Central to his argument is the need for preemptive **ethical frameworks** and safety measures to govern AI development, ensuring that such technologies align with human values and interests.

Beyond the immediate concerns of AI safety, Bostrom's work delves into broader philosophical inquiries, such as the **simulation hypothesis**, which postulates that reality as we perceive it could be an artificial simulation. This hypothesis, alongside his discussions on human enhancement technologies, invites readers to reconsider the very nature of existence and humanity's place within a potentially malleable reality.

David Chalmers's contributions to the philosophy of mind, particularly his articulation of the **"hard problem"** of consciousness, offer a complementary perspective to the technological focus of Bostrom's work. Chalmers posits that understanding the subjective experience of consciousness remains an unresolved puzzle, a challenge that gains new dimensions in the context of artificial intelligence. His exploration of consciousness intersects with AI advancements, raising profound questions about the possibility of conscious machines and the ethical implications thereof. His speculative engagement with the notion of a **simulated reality** further enriches the discourse, prompting readers to contemplate the philosophical ramifications of living within a construct that blurs the lines between the artificial and the real.

By juxtaposing Bostrom's focus on existential risk and AI safety with Chalmers's inquiries into consciousness and reality, readers have a multifaceted perspective on the ethical and existential challenges of technological advancement. This exploration not only highlights the critical importance of philosophical inquiry in the age of technology but also showcases the need for a nuanced understanding of how AI might reshape the human condition. Through their work, Bostrom and Chalmers illuminate the path forward, advocating for a future where technological progress is guided by deep ethical consideration and a stringent devotion to the enhancement of human well-being and freedom.

## Biotechnology and the Redefinition of Human Life

Biotechnology, encompassing fields such as **genetic engineering** and **synthetic biology**, presents another arena of ethical inquiry, challenging traditional conceptions of life, identity, and human enhancement. The possibility of genetically modifying human embryos, for instance, raises profound questions about the ethics of enhancement, the nature of **human identity**, and the rights of future generations. Philosophers like **Jürgen Habermas** and **Francis Fukuyama** have critically examined the implications of biotechnological advancements, warning against a future in which human nature becomes a malleable project subject to technological manipulation. These discussions illustrate the need for a robust ethical framework that can address the complexities introduced by biotechnological innovations, ensuring that such technologies are developed and applied in a manner that respects human dignity and autonomy.

Jürgen Habermas is a critical voice exploring the intersections of ethics, technology, and democracy within the fabric of modern society. His prolific body of work, which spans the intricacies of **communicative action** to the foundations of the public sphere, offers a compelling framework for understanding the challenges and opportunities presented by technological advancements in the contemporary world. His contributions to the dialogue on technology and ethics are anchored in his deep commitment to the ideals of **rational discourse** and **democratic deliberation**. In the face of increasing technological complexity, Habermas advocates for a societal model that prioritizes **transparent communication** and **participatory democracy**, viewing these principles as essential to navigating the ethical quandaries posed by innovations such as biotechnology and digital media. His concept of the "**lifeworld**," as articulated in "**The Theory of Communicative Action**," emphasizes the importance of maintaining a vibrant public sphere where citizens can engage in reasoned debate about the direction of technological progress and its impact on society.

Simultaneously, Francis Fukuyama's exploration of the ethical implications of technological advancements, particularly in the realms of **genetics** and **biotechnology**, positions him as a central figure in contemporary philosophical debates. His seminal work, "**Our Posthuman Future: Consequences of the Biotechnology Revolution**," dives into the profound questions raised by the potential for human enhancement and genetic modification, challenging readers to consider the implications of altering the very essence of human nature. Fukuyama argues that such technologies, while holding the promise of eradicating disease and enhancing human capabilities, also pose significant risks to the fundamental principles of equality and dignity that underpin democratic societies. He warns of a future where the unchecked application of biotechnological enhancements could lead to new forms of inequality and potentially erode the shared humanity that grounds ethical and political discourse. Fukuyama's call for **regulatory frameworks** and **ethical guidelines** to govern the use of biotechnology reflects a broader concern for ensuring that technological advancements serve to enhance, rather than undermine, the fabric of human society.

## Digital Privacy and the Right to Autonomy

The digital revolution has radically transformed the world of **privacy**, **surveillance**, and **information exchange**. The collection and analysis of vast amounts of personal data by governments and corporations pose significant threats to individual autonomy and the right to privacy. Philosophers like **Helen Nissenbaum** and **Shoshana Zuboff** have explored the ethical dimensions of digital privacy, emphasizing the importance of consent, transparency, and control over personal information in the digital age. These discussions highlight the challenges of safeguarding autonomy and privacy rights in a world where digital technologies permeate every aspect of life, calling for rigorous ethical standards and regulatory frameworks to protect individuals in the digital realm.

Helen Nissenbaum's concept of "**contextual integrity**," a foundational principle articulated in her book "**Privacy in Context: Technology, Policy, and the Integrity of Social Life**," provides a robust framework for understanding and evaluating privacy in an age dominated by digital information flows. Nissenbaum argues that **privacy norms are context-dependent**, varying across different social settings, and that breaches of privacy occur when these implicit norms are violated, regardless of the sensitivity of the data involved. Her work extends beyond theoretical discourse, engaging with **practical policy implications** and the **design of information technologies**. She champions a nuanced approach to privacy that respects the complexity of social contexts, advocating for technology and policy solutions that uphold the contextual integrity of personal information. In addressing the challenges posed by surveillance, data mining, and other digital practices, Nissenbaum's insights show the importance of maintaining ethical standards that protect individuals' rights to privacy and autonomy in the digital landscape.

Shoshana Zuboff's seminal contributions to understanding the intersection of technology, capitalism, and society are encapsulated in her groundbreaking work "**The Age of Surveillance Capitalism**." Zuboff introduces the concept of "**surveillance capitalism**," a new economic order that claims human experience as free raw material for hidden commercial practices of **extraction, prediction**, and **sales**. She meticulously outlines how technology companies, through the mass collection and analysis of personal data, have created a pervasive system of surveillance that poses unprecedented threats to individual autonomy and democracy. Zuboff's analysis explores the mechanisms by which surveillance capitalism undermines traditional notions of privacy and reshapes the social fabric. She calls for a collective awakening to the dangers of **unchecked data collection** and **algorithmic manipulation**, urging societies to reclaim the digital future through legal and social reforms that ensure technology serves the public good. Her work not only provides a critical examination of the present technological landscape but also offers a visionary perspective on the potential for reclaiming digital spaces for empowerment and democratic participation.

The philosophical responses to technological change reflect a critical engagement with the ethical and political challenges posed by the rapid evolution of technology. These advancements, while offering immense potential for improving human life, also introduce dilemmas that necessitate a rethinking of fundamental ethical principles and political institutions. The exploration of these issues underscores the urgency of developing philosophical frameworks that can navigate the complexities of the technological age, ensuring that advancements in AI, biotechnology, and digital technologies enhance human well-being and freedom, rather than undermining them. As we stand at the crossroads of technological innovation and ethical responsibility, the discourse on moral and political philosophy becomes ever more vital in guiding the trajectory of human progress.

# VI. Globalization and Multiculturalism

The dawn of the 21st century has been riddled with an unprecedented acceleration of globalization, driven by technological advancements that have bound the world into a tightly interconnected web of cultural and economic exchanges. This phenomenon of increased **global interconnectedness** brings to the fore complex philosophical questions about identity, justice, and ethics in a multicultural world. In this section we navigate the philosophical responses to these technological changes, focusing on the concepts of **cosmopolitanism**, **global justice**, and the intricate balance between **universal human rights** and **cultural relativism**.

## Cosmopolitanism

Cosmopolitanism, with its roots in Stoic philosophy, has re-emerged as a compelling ethical stance in response to globalization. It posits the idea that all human beings, irrespective of national, cultural, or religious affiliations, belong to a single community governed by shared moral laws. Contemporary philosophers like **Kwame Anthony Appiah** and **Martha Nussbaum** have championed cosmopolitanism, advocating for a global sense of solidarity and ethical responsibility. This perspective encourages a reevaluation of nationalistic and **parochial attitudes**, urging a commitment to global justice and the common good.

Kwame Anthony Appiah champions **global citizenship** and the ethical consideration of all human beings irrespective of nationality, culture, or religion. In "**Cosmopolitanism: Ethics in a World of Strangers**," Appiah navigates the complexities of cultural diversity and globalization, proposing a philosophy that emphasizes shared human values while recognizing and respecting cultural differences. Her cosmopolitanism is grounded in the belief that human beings have obligations to each other that transcend local affiliations and loyalties. He argues for a world where individuals can engage across cultural divides with respect and openness, fostering dialogue and understanding. His approach to ethics is notable for its emphasis on conversation as a means of bridging differences, suggesting that mutual respect and understanding are achievable, even in the face of profound diversity. Moreover, Appiah challenges the notion of **fixed identities**, arguing instead for a fluid understanding of self that accommodates multiple affiliations and evolves over time. This perspective on identity is crucial for navigating the multicultural perspectives of contemporary societies, offering a pathway to **coexistence** that values diversity as a source of richness rather than division.

Martha Nussbaum's contributions to moral and political philosophy are extensive, with a particular focus on justice, ethics, and human development. Her "**capabilities approach**," developed in collaboration with economist **Amartya Sen**, provides a framework for evaluating human well-being and social justice that goes beyond traditional metrics of economic prosperity. Nussbaum's work is deeply concerned with what it means to live a **life worthy of human dignity**, emphasizing the importance of enabling individuals to realize their potential and make meaningful choices.

In "**Creating Capabilities: The Human Development Approach**," Nussbaum outlines a list of fundamental human capabilities, such as life, health, education, and political participation, arguing that a just society should aim to enhance these capabilities for all its members. Her approach shifts the focus of ethical and political inquiry from the distribution of resources to the quality of life that individuals are able to lead, advocating for policies and institutions that support human flourishing. Nussbaum also addresses the challenges of global justice, arguing that the capabilities approach has universal applicability and can guide international efforts to **address inequality**, **poverty**, and **oppression**. Her vision of global ethics calls for a recognition of shared humanity and a commitment to fostering human capabilities across cultural and national boundaries.

Kwame Anthony Appiah and Martha Nussbaum's combined insights offer a compelling vision for contemporary society, one that balances respect for diversity with the pursuit of universal ethical principles. By championing dialogue, mutual understanding, and the enhancement of human capabilities, Appiah and Nussbaum contribute to a framework for global ethics that is both inclusive and empowering.

## Global Justice and the Ethics of Interconnectedness

The discourse on global justice has gained momentum in light of the inequalities exacerbated by globalization. Philosophers such as **Thomas Pogge** and **Amartya Sen** have contributed significantly to this debate, examining the ethical obligations of affluent nations towards those disadvantaged by the global economic system.

Pogge's work is characterized by a rigorous analysis of the global economic order and its impact on the world's most vulnerable populations. Pogge argues that many of the existing international policies and practices exacerbate poverty and hinder the realization of human rights. His major work, **"World Poverty and Human Rights**," challenges the ethical foundations of the current global system, asserting that affluent countries and their citizens bear significant moral responsibility for perpetuating economic injustices through their support of coercive global institutions. Pogge's proposal for a global resources dividend represents a practical mechanism for addressing these injustices, suggesting that nations should contribute a portion of their resource and pollution space revenues to fund global **poverty** alleviation efforts. This innovative approach underscores Pogge's commitment to transforming the structures that underpin global inequality, advocating for a world order that prioritizes the dignity and rights of all individuals.

Amartya Sen, a Nobel laureate in Economics, has significantly influenced the discourse on justice, development, and human capabilities. Sen's **"capabilities approach"** offers a powerful alternative to traditional welfare economics, focusing on what individuals are actually able to do and to be – in other words, their capabilities. Unlike approaches that measure well-being solely in terms of economic output or subjective happiness, Sen emphasizes the importance of freedom and opportunity in achieving a life one has **reason to value**. In works such as **"Development as Freedom**," Sen articulates a vision of development that is inherently linked to the expansion of human freedoms, arguing that economic growth should be assessed by its impact on people's lives and capabilities. This perspective not only shifts the focus of **development policies** but also highlights the role of public participation and **social choice** in determining the paths to justice and well-being.

Together, their work invites readers to engage deeply with the complexities of global justice, encouraging a move beyond simplistic solutions towards a more nuanced understanding of the ethical imperatives at play. By integrating the insights of Pogge and Sen, we inspire a reimagined approach to building a world that respects the **dignity and capabilities of all its inhabitants**. Through their visionary work, Pogge and Sen contribute to a foundational shift in how we conceive of and strive for justice in an interconnected world, providing a beacon of hope and a call to action for philosophers, policymakers, and global citizens alike.

## The Tension Between Universal Rights and Cultural Relativism

As societies become more multicultural, the tension between universal human rights and cultural relativism has become increasingly pronounced. This debate centers on whether moral principles and rights are universally applicable or whether they are contingent on cultural contexts. Philosophers such as **Seyla Benhabib** and **Charles Taylor** have navigated these contentious waters, seeking a middle ground that respects cultural diversity while upholding fundamental ethical standards.

Seyla Benhabib, a prominent philosopher and political theorist, has made significant contributions to our understanding of **democracy**, **ethics**, and the **rights of individuals** in the context of global interdependence. Her work on the ethics of **immigration**, the rights of **minorities**, and **transnational citizenship** challenges traditional notions of sovereignty and national identity. In **"The Rights of Others: Aliens, Residents, and Citizens,"** Benhabib advocates for a cosmopolitanism rooted in the principles of universal respect and **egalitarian reciprocity**. She argues for democratic iterations; ongoing, participatory dialogues that allow for the negotiation of differences and the reinterpretation of universal human rights within diverse cultural contexts. Benhabib's philosophy tells of the importance of ethical dialogue in navigating the complexities of modern pluralistic societies. Her emphasis on deliberative democracy and the inclusion of marginalized voices contributes to a more nuanced understanding of justice and human rights, advocating for policies and practices that reflect the interwoven fabric of our shared global community.

Charles Taylor's explorations of **identity, modernity**, and **secularism** have significantly shaped contemporary thought on the politics of recognition and the challenges of multiculturalism. His seminal essay **"Multiculturalism and 'The Politics of Recognition'"** examines the demands of cultural groups for recognition of their unique identities by the broader society. Taylor argues that **non-recognition** or **misrecognition** can inflict harm, marginalizing individuals and preventing them from participating fully in society. He advocates for a model of politics that acknowledges and respects the diversity of cultural expressions and identities within a framework of dialogical interactions. Taylor's contributions extend to his analysis of the **secular age**, questioning how societies can maintain a sense of moral order and common good amidst **growing religious** and **philosophical pluralism**. His work calls for an open, pluralistic public sphere where various beliefs and values can coexist, fostering a shared commitment to the collective welfare while respecting individual differences.

The philosophical responses to technological changes, globalization, and multiculturalism outlined in this section portray the complex ethical terrain of our interconnected era. The concepts of cosmopolitanism, global justice, and the dialectic between universalism and relativism provide critical lenses through which to examine the philosophical implications of our globalized reality.

These discussions not only enrich our understanding of moral and political philosophy in the contemporary world but also guide us toward more equitable, respectful, and interconnected global societies. As we navigate the challenges and opportunities presented by globalization, the philosophical insights explored here serve as beacons, illuminating paths toward a more just and harmonious global community.

These philosophical insights provide crucial guidance for contemporary governance, suggesting that ethical leadership in a globalized world involves a commitment to dialogue, transparency, and inclusivity. It requires policies that not only acknowledge the interdependence of the global community but actively leverage this interconnectedness to develop conditions that promote human flourishing across all societies. This includes rethinking how laws and policies can be formulated to reflect a shared human dignity while being adaptable to local contexts and cultural specificities.

Overall, the philosophical exploration of globalization and multiculturalism reveals a vast array of perspectives that challenge and expand our ethical ideas. By engaging with these philosophical debates, we learn to traverse the moral complexities of an interconnected world. We are encouraged to build bridges across cultural and national divides, nourishing a global community that respects diversity while striving towards common ethical goals. This dialogue is not only about enhancing our understanding of global justice, cosmopolitanism, and cultural respect but also about actively shaping a world where every individual can partake in the dignity and justice that they are due. Through this philosophical journey, we contribute to the ongoing endeavor to understand and respond to the unique challenges of our time, aiming for a future that is just, equitable, and respectful of the human culture.

# Chapter 9: Contemporary Challenges & Innovations

As we stand at the threshold of the 21st century, confronting a constellation of unprecedented global challenges, the enduring legacy of moral and political philosophy becomes ever more evident. From the rich discourses of the Greek Philosophical Era to the profound reflections of Modern and Postmodern thinkers, the journey of moral and political thought has been one of continuous evolution, adaptation, and profound insight into the human condition. In our continuing discourse on moral and political philosophy we aim to explore a forward-looking perspective, rummaging together the historical narrative of philosophical inquiry with the pressing exigencies of our times.

Today, the world grapples with deep-seated inequalities, the ethics of migration, the sustainability of the environment, and the resilience of democratic institutions amid rising populism and authoritarian tendencies. These challenges demand a reinvigorated engagement with moral and political philosophy, not merely as an academic exercise, but as a vital compass guiding action and policy in an uncertain world.

We need to look up to and engage with philosophers like Elizabeth Anderson and Martha Nussbaum, who have pioneered innovative approaches to understanding inequality and justice, emphasizing the importance of capabilities and access to opportunities as fundamental measures of a just society, illustrating the role of philosophy in critiquing existing social and economic structures and envisioning alternatives that prioritize human dignity and well-being. The use of Martha Nussbaum's Capabilities Approach in the UN's Human Development Index showcases how philosophical frameworks influence global policy.

As we scrutinize the influence of moral and political philosophy on these issues, a critical area of focus must be the philosophical underpinnings of our education systems. Education does not merely equip individuals with knowledge; it fundamentally shapes the social and moral fabric of society. The debates over the nature and purpose of education, from the liberal arts education advocating for a well-rounded, critically thinking individual to vocational training designed to meet economic demands, reflect deeper philosophical questions about the kind of citizens we aim to cultivate.

Philosophical discussions on education often revolve around its role in democracy. Philosophers such as John Dewey have argued that education is not only about personal enrichment but is essential for the functioning of a democratic society. It prepares individuals to participate fully and effectively as citizens, equipped with the skills to think critically, debate, and engage in the civic life of their communities. Moreover, the deliberation over the purpose of education whether to foster individual autonomy, promote social justice, or ensure economic productivity, raises significant questions about the values that encapsulate our educational institutions. The role of education in cultivating a just and informed citizenry invites us to consider how curricula and educational structures either perpetuate inequality or promote inclusivity. Philosophical engagement with education thus becomes a pivotal arena for advancing debates on social justice, equity, and the nurturing of democratic virtues.

The future of democracy, in the face of emerging technologies, shifting global power dynamics, and existential environmental threats, remains a critical area of philosophical exploration. The work of Jürgen Habermas on the public sphere and deliberative democracy offers valuable insights into fostering inclusive, reasoned discourse as the foundation of democratic life. Simultaneously, the rise of digital platforms and the challenges of misinformation and polarization highlight the need for philosophical engagement with the principles of dialogue, truth, and the common good. Again, in discussions about AI ethics, proponents of strict AI regulations are often in opposition to those advocating for a laissez-faire approach to technological development, arguing that over-regulation could hinder technological advancement and economic growth. These discussions accentuate the application of ethical frameworks in AI, such as IEEE's adoption of ethical considerations proposed by philosophers in its guidelines for autonomous and intelligent systems, demonstrating the role of philosophy in technological governance.

Amidst the complexity of modern challenges, philosophical innovation emerges as a beacon of hope and direction. The incorporation of digital ethics, spearheaded by thinkers like Luciano Floridi, reflects an acute awareness of the moral dimensions of technological advancement. As artificial intelligence, big data, and digital surveillance become embedded in the fabric of daily life, philosophical inquiry into the nature of privacy, autonomy, and the human self gains renewed urgency. In contrast, digital ethics, particularly regarding data privacy, confront objections related to feasibility and the risk of stifling innovation.

Moreover, the COVID-19 pandemic has starkly highlighted the need for a philosophical examination of health ethics on a worldwide scale. This examination explores issues such as equitable access to healthcare, the responsibilities of wealthy nations towards lower-income countries, and the ethics underlying global health initiatives. Philosophers like Norman Daniels have long debated the just allocation of health resources, arguing for health equity as a fundamental aspect of justice. Global health ethics also confronts the balance between individual rights and public health needs, especially vivid during health crises such as pandemics. The enforcement of quarantines, vaccination mandates, and travel restrictions raises critical ethical questions about the extent to which individual freedoms can be curtailed for the greater good. Philosophical debates in this area explore the tension between utilitarian principles, which justify actions that maximize overall well-being, and deontological ethics, which emphasize the intrinsic rights and dignity of individuals.

Furthermore, the philosophical discourse on global health ethics urges us to consider how values like empathy, solidarity, and reciprocity should inform international health policies. The concept of 'health as a global public good' proposed by thinkers such as Lawrence Gostin, calls for an ethical framework that transcends national borders, advocating for global cooperation in the face of health emergencies. This approach not only challenges the international community to rethink health policy but also to embody the philosophical ideals of global justice and equity in practical responses to health crises.

The ethics of migration, a topic that Seyla Benhabib and others have explored in depth, presents a test case for the principles of cosmopolitanism and global justice. As millions seek refuge from conflict, persecution, and poverty, the philosophical discourse on rights, sovereignty, and global responsibility becomes directly implicated in the formulation of humane and ethical policies that respect the dignity of migrants and refugees. However, cosmopolitan theories of global justice have been critiqued for potentially undermining the sovereignty and cultural integrity of nations.

Furthermore, the environmental crisis has catalyzed a philosophical renaissance in ecocentric ethics and the exploration of humanity's relationship with the natural world. Philosophers like Bruno Latour and Vandana Shiva advocate for a radical rethinking of human exceptionalism, promoting a vision of coexistence that honors the interdependence of all life forms and addresses the ecological imperatives of sustainability and resilience. In contrast, the anthropocentric viewpoint directly opposes the ecocentric views. While ecocentrists argue for a biocentric equality, proponents of anthropocentrism defend the pragmatic need for human-centered policies.

Our philosophical journey is thus connected through a millennia of philosophical inquiry, from the agora of ancient Athens to the digital forums of the modern age. Each era, with its distinct challenges and innovations, contributes to a richer understanding of the possibilities and responsibilities of human coexistence. As we walk the uncertainties of the postmodern era, the historical imperative of moral and political philosophy endures, offering guidance, inspiration, and a framework for imagining a world marked by justice, compassion, and shared human flourishing.

As we conclude this exploration of contemporary challenges through the lens of moral and political philosophy, we have engaged with a diverse array of pressing issues, from the ethics of migration and digital privacy to the dilemmas posed by global health crises and environmental sustainability. Yet, it is clear that our discourse has merely scratched the surface of the complex, multifaceted problems facing modern societies. The very presence of these challenges should not be seen solely in a negative light; rather, it signals a maturing of societal consciousness, akin to a medical advancement that allows for better diagnosis of previously undetected ailments. Just as medicine cannot treat what it does not first diagnosed, so too must our philosophical inquiries lay bare the ethical and political "diseases" of our time before we can hope to remedy them.

In this spirit, our philosophical journey is both diagnostic and therapeutic. It is a process that seeks to uncover and understand the underlying issues that ail our societies, providing not just a critique but also a pathway to healing. By continuing to question, analyze, and debate, we not only illuminate the problems at hand but also begin to forge solutions that promote a healthier, more just, and flourishing human collective. The discourse does not end with this chapter or even this book; it is an ongoing, ever-evolving conversation that each generation must engage in if we are to progress towards a more enlightened and humane world. In this expansive philosophical endeavor, we diagnose, we treat, and we aspire to cure, not out of naïve optimism but from a steadfast commitment to the betterment of humanity.

# Epilogue

As we conclude this exploration through the history of western moral philosophy and ethics, it's essential to reflect on the enduring significance of our philosophical heritage and its unrelenting relevance to our current world. This book has traversed through the ebbs and flows of philosophical thought, from the ancient dialogues that grappled with the fundamentals of human nature to the sophisticated debates of modern times addressing the complexities of technology, justice, and ethical governance. Our journey, however, is far from complete.

The chapters of this book have not only recounted a history of ideas but have also invited us to engage with these ideas actively, to question deeply, and to contemplate the role of philosophy in the very essence of our daily lives. As we stand in an era marked by unprecedented technological advancement and complex global challenges, the insights from the past are not just historical footnotes but are vital tools for navigating our present and shaping our future.

Philosophy teaches us the art of questioning and the virtue of doubt, encouraging a skeptical inquiry into the narratives we live by and the values we hold dear. It challenges us to look beyond the superficiality of prevailing trends and to engage with the deeper currents of human thought. Each philosophical era we've explored offers unique perspectives that are crucial for understanding the multifaceted nature of human existence and for addressing the existential questions that persist through time.

As we move forward, the dialogues between the great thinkers of the past and the pressing issues of today should continue to evolve. The discourse on moral and political philosophy is particularly crucial as we confront ethical dilemmas in bioethics, environmental stewardship, and global justice. These are not merely academic exercises but are imperative for the well-being and sustainability of our global community.

In embracing the philosophical journey, we are also tasked with the responsibility of translating philosophical inquiry into actionable insights that can inform policy, guide ethical decision-making, and foster a more just and compassionate world. Philosophy empowers us not only to think critically but to act thoughtfully. As we engage with the philosophical dimensions of contemporary issues, let us be guided by the wisdom of the past, the urgency of the now, and the promise of the future.

Let this book serve as a catalyst for further reflection and discussion, inviting each reader to contribute to the ongoing dialogue of philosophy in their unique way. May we all continue to seek wisdom, cultivate virtue, and pursue the common good. Philosophy, after all, is not just a discipline to be studied; it is a way of life to be lived.

As we close this chapter, let us carry forward the spirit of inquiry and the courage to confront new challenges with philosophical rigor and ethical commitment. Let us shape a world that reflects our deepest values and highest aspirations, informed by philosophical thought that has been laid before us. Let the journey continue.

# Glossary

1. **Agency**: The ability of individuals to act autonomously in making moral or political decisions.
2. **Aristotelianism**: The philosophy of Aristotle, emphasizing empirical observation and the integration of all human knowledge.
3. **Atomism**: The theory that all matter consists of tiny, indivisible particles.
4. **Causality**: The relationship between cause and effect.
5. **Compatibilism**: The belief that free will and determinism are mutually compatible.
6. **Consequentialism**: Ethical theories that judge actions based on their outcomes.
7. **Constructivism**: The theory that knowledge is constructed, not discovered.
8. **Cosmopolitanism**: The ideology that all human beings belong to a single community, based on a shared morality.
9. **Deconstruction:** A method of critical analysis of philosophical and literary language which emphasizes the internal workings of language and conceptual systems, the relational quality of meaning, and the assumptions implicit in forms of expression.
10. **Deontological**: Ethical theories that emphasize duties and rules.
11. **Determinism**: The doctrine that all events, including human actions, are ultimately determined by causes external to the will.
12. **Dialectics**: The art of investigating or discussing the truth of opinions.
13. **Dualism**: The division of something conceptually into two opposed or contrasted aspects.
14. **Egalitarianism**: The principle that all people are equal and deserve equal rights and opportunities.
15. **Empiricism**: The theory that all knowledge is derived from sense
16. **Epistemology**: The theory of knowledge, especially with regard to its methods, validity, and scope.
17. **Ethical**: The belief that morality varies between individuals and cultures and that there are no absolute moral truths.
18. **Existentialism**: A philosophical theory focusing on individual freedom, choice, and existence.
19. **Feminism**: The advocacy of women's rights on the ground of the equality of the sexes.
20. **Free**: The power of acting without the constraint of necessity or fate.
21. **Hedonism**: The ethical theory that pleasure is the highest good and proper aim of human life.
22. **Hermeneutics**: The theory and methodology of interpretation, especially of scriptural texts.
23. **Humanism**: A rationalist outlook or system of thought attaching prime importance to human rather than divine or supernatural matters.
24. **Idealism**: The practice of forming or pursuing ideals, especially unrealistically.
25. **Immaterialism**: The doctrine that there are no material substances; everything is immaterial.
26. **Incompatibilism**: The belief that free will and determinism are logically incompatible.
27. **Individualism**: The principle of being independent and self
28. Instrumentalism: A pragmatic philosophical approach that views concepts and theories as merely useful instruments.
29. **Intuitionism**: The doctrine that moral truths are known by intuition.

30. **Liberalism**: A political and moral philosophy based on liberty, consent of the governed, and equality before the law.
31. **Materialism**: The belief that only physical matter exists and that everything, including thought, feeling, mind, and will, can be explained in terms of matter and physical phenomena.
32. **Metaphysics**: The branch of philosophy that deals with the first principles of things, including abstract concepts such as being, knowing, identity, time, and space.
33. **Moral**: The ethical belief that there are absolute standards against which moral questions can be judged.
34. **Natural**: A body of unchanging moral principles regarded as a basis for all human conduct.
35. **Nihilism**: The rejection of all religious and moral principles, often in the belief that life is meaningless.
36. **Nominalism**: The doctrine that universals or general ideas are mere names without any corresponding reality.
37. **Objectivism**: The belief that certain things, especially moral truths, exist independently of human knowledge or perception of them.
38. **Ontology**: The branch of metaphysics dealing with the nature of being.
39. **Pantheism**: The belief that reality is identical with divinity, or that all
40. **Phenomenology**: The philosophical study of the structures of experience and consciousness.
41. **Platonism**: The philosophy of Plato or his followers.
42. **Political**: The study of fundamental questions about the state, government, politics, liberty, justice, and the enforcement of a legal code.
43. **Pragmatism**: A philosophical approach that assesses the truth of meaning of theories or beliefs in terms of the success of their practical application.
44. **Rationalism**: A belief or theory that opinions and actions should be based on reason and knowledge rather than on religious belief or emotional response.
45. **Realism**: The attitude or practice of accepting a situation as it is and being prepared to deal with it accordingly.
46. **Relativism**: The doctrine that knowledge, truth, and morality exist in relation to culture, society, or historical context, and are not absolute.
47. **Skepticism**: A skeptical attitude; doubt as to the truth of something.
48. **Social**: An implicit agreement among the members of a society to cooperate for social benefits.
49. **Solipsism**: The view or theory that the self is all that can be known to exist.
50. **Stoicism**: The endurance of pain or hardship without the display of feelings and without complaint.
51. **Teleology**: The explanation or study of phenomena in terms of the purpose they serve rather than of the cause by which they arise; often associated with Aristotelian philosophy.
52. **Utilitarianism**: The doctrine that actions are right if they are useful or for the benefit of a majority.
53. **Virtue Ethics:** An approach to ethics that emphasizes the character of the moral agent, rather than rules or consequences, as the key element of ethical thinking.

# List of References and Further Readings

- **Aquinas**, T. Summa Theologica.
- **Arendt**, H. The Origins of Totalitarianism.
- **Aristotle**. Nicomachean Ethics.
- **Bauman**, Z. Liquid Modernity.
- **Beauvoir**, S. de. The Second Sex.
- **Bentham**, J. Introduction to the Principles of Morals and Legislation.
- **Burke**, E. Reflections on the Revolution in France.
- **Camus**, A. The Myth of Sisyphus.
- **Derrida**, J. Of Grammatology.
- **Descartes**, R. Meditations on First Philosophy.
- **Dewey**, J. Democracy and Education.
- **Dworkin**, R. Law's Empire.
- **Foucault**, M. Discipline and Punish: The Birth of the Prison.
- **Habermas**, J. The Theory of Communicative Action.
- **Hegel**, G. W. F. Philosophy of Right.
- **Heidegger**, M. Being and Time.
- **Hobbes**, T. Leviathan.
- **Husserl**, E. Cartesian Meditations.
- **Hume**, D. A Treatise of Human Nature.
- **Kant**, I. Critique of Pure Reason.
- **Kuhn**, T. S. The Structure of Scientific Revolutions.
- **Levinas**, E. Totality and Infinity.
- **Locke**, J. Two Treatises of Government.
- **Lyotard**, J.-F. The Postmodern Condition.
- **Machiavelli**, N. The Prince.
- **Marx**, K. Das Kapital.
- **Merleau**-Ponty, M. Phenomenology of Perception.
- **Mill**, J. S. On Liberty.
- **Nietzsche**, F. Beyond Good and Evil.
- **Peirce**, C. S. Philosophical Writings of Peirce.
- **Plato**. Republic.
- **Popper**, K. The Logic of Scientific Discovery.
- **Quine**, W. V. Word and Object.
- **Rawls**, J. A Theory of Justice.
- **Rousseau**, J.-J. The Social Contract.
- **Sartre**, J.-P. Being and Nothingness.
- **Schmitt**, C. Political Theology.
- **Smith**, A. The Wealth of Nations.
- **Spinoza**, B. Ethics.
- **Tariq**, W. Probing Freewill.
- **Wittgenstein**, L. Philosophical Investigations.
- **Žižek**, S. The Sublime Object of Ideology.

Printed in Great Britain
by Amazon

2138bb2d-6950-412f-84fd-5fd43357a919R02